THE DISCERNING TRAVELER'S GUIDE TO ROMANTIC HIDEAWAYS OF THE EAST COAST

THE

DISCERNING TRAVELER'S GUIDE TO ROMANTIC HIDEAWAYS OF THE EAST COAST

DAVID AND LINDA GLICKSTEIN

Drawings by Jane Adams Stauffer
Maps by David Glickstein

St. Martin's Press
New York

Drawings by Jane Adams Stauffer
Maps by David Glickstein
Design by Chris Welch

Library of Congress Cataloging-in-Publication Data

Glickstein, David.
The discerning traveler's guide to romantic hideaways of the East Coast / David and Linda Glickstein.
p. cm.
ISBN 0-312-09272-5 (pbk.)
1. Hotels, taverns, etc.—United States—Atlantic Coast—Guidebooks. 2. Bed and breakfast accommodations—United States—Atlantic Coast—Guidebooks. 3. Atlantic Coast (U.S.)—Guidebooks.
I. Glickstein, Linda. II. Title.
TX907.3.A86G57   1993
647.947501—dc20   93-475
CIP

First Edition: June 1993
10 9 8 7 6 5 4 3 2 1

In memory of Nancy Glickstein

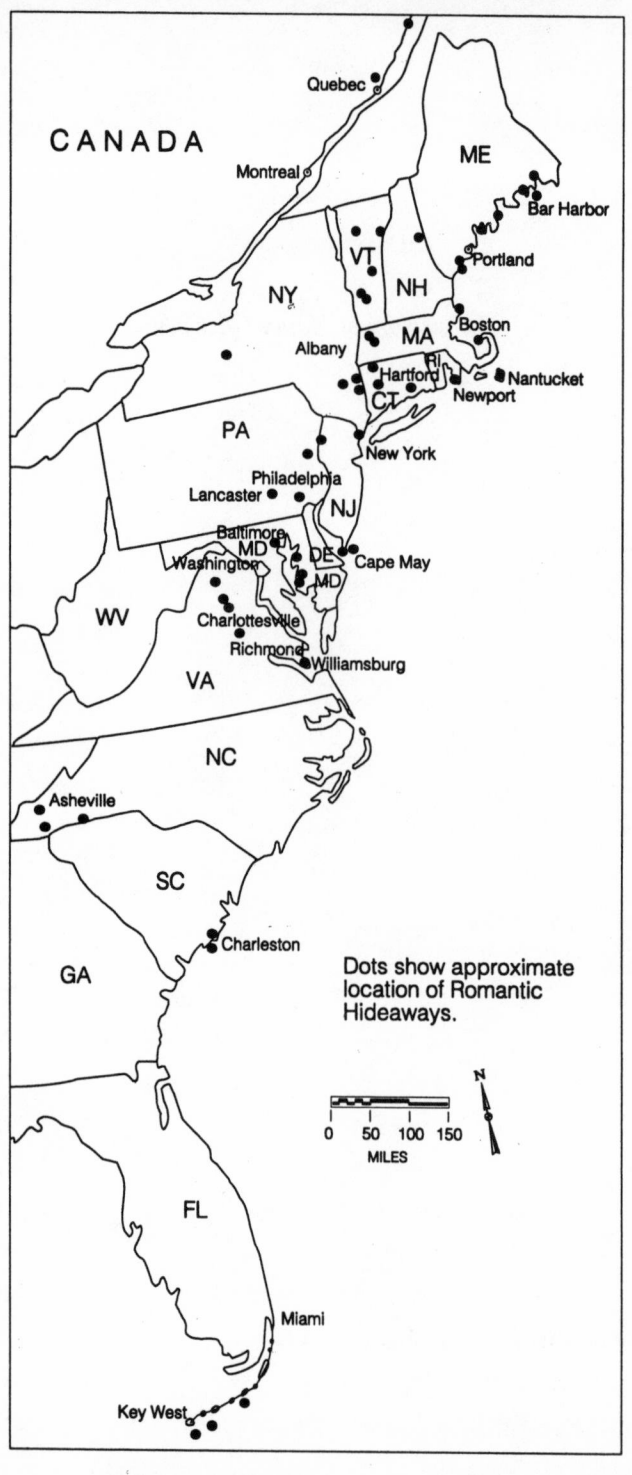

Dots show approximate location of Romantic Hideaways.

CONTENTS

INTRODUCTION

Close your eyes and imagine your ideal romantic hideaway. To some, this means a small inn, warm and cozy with a working fireplace, crisp linens, plush pillows, and a canopy bed. To others, it is formal elegance with expansive rooms, a panoramic view of the mountains, and formal dining. Some see a quiet porch with rocking chairs and a view of a colorful sunset over the water; others relish sleeping late, luxuriating in a whirlpool tub, and enjoying a gourmet breakfast served in front of the fireplace. You might find the excitement of a city at your doorstep enticing, or you might prefer a remote location with more rustic facilities and the undeveloped splendor of thick forests and untouched shorelines.

A truly great inn, hotel, or resort is not just a package of amenities, a list of ingredients mixed and spread in certain proportions. Each place in this book has intangible as well as tangible aspects that create a unique experience. At its best, innkeeping is a commitment, an ideal, a striving for perfection. Many of the hostelries we describe are virtual museums of treasured antiques and artifacts, the result of years of passionate collecting.

Sharing a few days with someone special is time and money well spent. The gifts of time, love, and caring are some of the most meaningful gifts you can give. An experience that you and your loved one have shared can never be taken away from you.

That is what this book is all about: a gift of romantic hideaways where you can create lasting memories.

Each of these hideaways has its own distinctive features. From fairy-tale houses and charming cottages to elegant grand hotels, all have picturesque settings that are sure to nurture the soul. No matter where you live or when you plan to travel, you're sure to find that special haven, that romantic hideaway right for you.

Listings are arranged by state or province, starting with the northernmost destination in Québec and ending with Key West, Florida. The maps on pages xvi, 92, and 173 show the location of each. The rates listed are for two persons per night, based on double occupancy. If there is a service charge, we list it, but state and local lodging taxes are additional. *Note:* All rates and prices for Canadian inns and restaurants are in Canadian dollars.

Helping you choose a place to stay, and to select the room that best suits your taste, is our first consideration. We've also included short sections on where to dine, what to do in the area, and how to get to each of these hideaways.

All of the places that we have selected were reviewed in issues of our newsletter, "The Discerning Traveler,"® based on our personal visits. The choice of inns was ours alone; no one has paid to be included in this book. Further information about the areas in which each of these inns, bed-and-breakfasts, and hotels are located can be found in issues of "The Discerning Traveler"® and two guidebooks, *The Discerning Traveler's Guide to New England* and *The Discerning Traveler's Guide to the Middle Atlantic States.* An appendix at the back of this book cross-references each inn to the appropriate book or issue of the newsletter.

We have made every attempt to verify prices, hours, and dates of operation at the time this book went to press. It always is wise to call ahead, however, as many of the inns and restaurants are small and subject to changes in management, prices, and policies.

Finding romantic hideaways is a continuing process. We welcome your suggestions of other romantic hideaways. Please send your thoughts to us at 504 West Mermaid Lane, Philadelphia, Pennsylvania 19118.

Happy travels,
David and Linda Glickstein

THE DISCERNING TRAVELER'S GUIDE TO ROMANTIC HIDEAWAYS OF THE EAST COAST

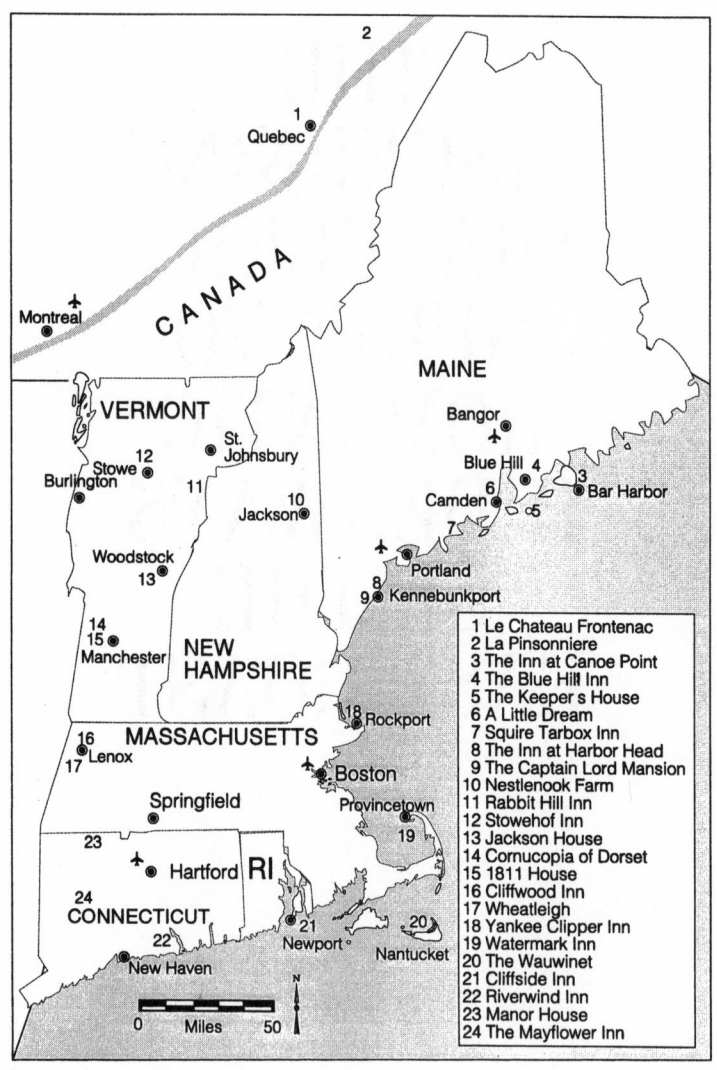

2 La Pinsonniere

1 Le Chateau Frontenac
2 La Pinsonniere
3 The Inn at Canoe Point
4 The Blue Hill Inn
5 The Keeper s House
6 A Little Dream
7 Squire Tarbox Inn
8 The Inn at Harbor Head
9 The Captain Lord Mansion
10 Nestlenook Farm
11 Rabbit Hill Inn
12 Stowehof Inn
13 Jackson House
14 Cornucopia of Dorset
15 1811 House
16 Cliffwood Inn
17 Wheatleigh
18 Yankee Clipper Inn
19 Watermark Inn
20 The Wauwinet
21 Cliffside Inn
22 Riverwind Inn
23 Manor House
24 The Mayflower Inn

CANADA

Montreal

Quebec 1

MAINE

VERMONT

St. Johnsbury

Bangor

Blue Hill 4
3
Bar Harbor
6
Camden 5
7

Stowe 12
Burlington
11
Jackson 10

Woodstock
13

NEW HAMPSHIRE

Portland
8
9 Kennebunkport

14
15
Manchester

MASSACHUSETTS

Rockport 18

Lenox 16
17

Boston

Springfield

Provincetown
19

23

Hartford RI

24
CONNECTICUT

22
New Haven

21
Newport

20
Nantucket

N

0 Miles 50

Le Château Frontenac, *Québec City, Québec*

This massive, castlelike, turreted hotel, made of stone and brick with green copper roofs, is recognized throughout the world. By the spring of 1993, $65 million worth of renovations and the addition of a four-story wing including an indoor pool, full-service health club, and 66 guest rooms will be complete.

All rooms have been redecorated with coordinated quilted bedspreads, upholstery, and draperies. In the main tower, the colors of the rugs, draperies, and fabrics are brighter and have more distinct patterns than one normally sees in hotels. Rooms have minibars, televisions, and telephones. As a general rule, the odd-numbered rooms overlook the St. Lawrence River and the even-numbered rooms overlook the city rooftops. The newest rooms are those on the eighteenth floor, a floor formerly used as maids' quarters. These rooms, accessible by a second elevator from the seventeenth floor, have dormer windows and high slanted ceilings. Referred to as the honeymoon rooms, they are the only ones with a double Jacuzzi in the bedroom. Other features include a queen-size bed and a bath with glass-walled shower, hair dryer, and second phone.

The spacious one- and two-bedroom suites located throughout the hotel offer stunning river views. One of the most unusual is an elegant duplex turret suite (# 6153), which has a living room on the lower level. Spiral stairs lead to the bedroom, which includes two queen-size beds, and a green-marble tiled bath with a kidney-shaped Jacuzzi and glass-walled shower.

Over the past two years, the hotel has also renovated its restaurants. Le Champlain is the most sumptuous and probably the most beautiful restaurant in the walled city (Upper Town). The service is polished and correct. Classic French cuisine is served in a plush carpeted, dark-paneled room with highback upholstered chairs. On weekends a harpist plays during dinner. Appetizers include such delicacies as Petrossian caviar, foie gras, lobster flan in a scallop mousse, local smoked salmon, and pheasant consommé with truffles.

For the main course, the traditional preparation of Dover sole in butter sauce is superb. Other choices include giant prawns flambéed in Pernod, tenderloin of buffalo with pepper sauce, an impressive chateaubriand with three sauces, and rack of lamb with Dijon herbs. For dessert, choose from an array of cakes or try the chilled Grand Marnier sabayon with a bowl of fresh fruit. Another option is the multi-course *dégustation* (a sampling of specialties) dinner, an excellent chance to try the best the chef has to offer.

The famous Sunday brunch at Le Champlain attracts the locals as well as the hotel guests to sample the attractively presented grand buffet. Brunch reservations are essential.

The recently opened Café de la Terrasse features large buffets throughout the day. Try to sit at one of the tables that face the Dufferin Terrace, directly in front of the hotel, where you can watch street musicians and passersby. Certain nights have themes, such as Italian on Thursday, fish and seafood on Friday, and dancing on Saturday night. The breakfast buffet is a good value.

The Bar St. Laurent, a large turret room with two fireplaces and a dance floor, has a new glass-enclosed area that overlooks Dufferin Terrace and the St. Lawrence River 200 feet below. This is one of our favorite spots.

Five hundred forty-four rooms and suites, all with private bath. Mid-May through mid-October and during winter carnival (February), rooms, $129–$230, suites, $195–$600. Other times of the year, rooms $104–$180, suites, $160–$475. Summer and winter packages available. Children under 18 free. No pets. Le Champlain: Dinner nightly (except Monday in low season), 6 to 9 P.M.; *dégustation* dinner (a sampling of specialties), $46.75, entrées, $18.75–$29.50. Café de la Terrasse: Breakfast buffet, $11.50, lunch buffet, $16.50, dinner buffet, $25–$32. A la carte available at all meals. Bar St. Laurent: Drinks nightly, dancing on weekends. 1 Rue des Carrières, Québec; (418) 692-3861; (800) 268-9420 (in Québec and Ontario only).

Where to Dine (apart from the Château). The plates at Laurie Raphaël arrived looking like sculpted works of art. For appetizers we had lobster meat wrapped in delicate phyllo pastry and served with a ginger vanilla dipping sauce. The red snapper filet was served with polenta and three kinds of wild mushrooms. The pastry chef prepares each dessert as the order is received. We had vanilla ice cream surrounded with fresh apricots and black currants, and rich chocolate crêpes cut into wide strips and served with chocolate sauce. 17 Rue Sault-au-Matelot; (418) 692-4555.

Stone walls, arches, and wood floors set the mood at Le Marie Clarisse (12 Rue du Petit Champlain; 418-692-0857) where fresh fish is the specialty. We started with lightly sautéed medallions of monkfish accompanied by slices of grilled apple and asparagus in an intense curry-flavored sauce. Thin braided strips of salmon were served on a bed of lemon-flavored bean sprouts. Stingray was grilled and arranged in a fan shape; grilled halibut was served with a light herbed cream sauce.

Serge Bruyère, the best known chef in Québec City, owns four restaurants covering all price ranges, and a gourmet shop located in an 1843 Upper Town building. La Grand Table is his flagship. We enjoyed delicately fried scallops paired with bean sprouts and soy sauce, and pieces of lobster served on fresh pasta with a tantalizing port and orange-cream sauce. A saddle of rabbit was served with rosemary and red peppers, and a thick rib of veal was prepared with herbs and black olives. Serge Bruyère Restaurants, 1200 Rue St. Jean; (418) 694-0618.

What to Do. Québec, settled in 1608, is the cradle of French civilization in North America. The designated historic district of Old Québec occupies 323 acres, which includes both the walled Upper Town and the Lower Town. The Upper Town, built on a massive rock promontory 200 feet above the St. Lawrence River, is surrounded by three miles of stone gates, ramparts, and cannon batteries. Roads, stairways, and a glass-walled funicular (cable-car elevator) connect the walled city with the Lower Town and the Old Port along the river.

For the visitor, Québec has its special charms throughout the year. In autumn the countryside is ablaze with color. Winter is frigid, with streets and buildings covered in snow, but hundreds of thousands join in the fun at the Carnival held each February. In summer, the city celebrates the warm weather with hanging baskets and window boxes overflowing with colorful flowers. Outdoor cafés are filled, and street performers entertain in public places. Visitors and residents alike stroll through the historic city well into the night. Don't be surprised to see a couple dancing on the Dufferin Terrace, accompanied by an accordion or fiddle, or to find a group of people singing along with a street musician. The way to experience Québec at any season is to slow down, enjoy the extraordinary cuisine, learn a few French words, and smile a lot. You will soon begin to feel the Québecois *joie de vivre*.

How to Get There. Québec City is about 150 miles northeast of Montreal. Take the New York State Thruway (I-87) to the Canadian border. Go east on Route 20 to Route 73. Cross the St. Lawrence River on the Québec Bridge. Turn east on Route 175 for five miles to Old Québec.

La Pinsonnière, *Cap-à-l'Aigle, Québec*

This deluxe inn and superb restaurant, about a ninety-minute drive east of Québec City, is located on a spectacular piece of land on a steep hill 200 feet above the rugged north shore of the St. Lawrence River. Only two of the five levels are visible from the front of the inn.

The inn has a quiet, sophisticated feeling. The lobby, common rooms, and restaurant are filled with the owners' fine collection of Québec art, some of which is for sale. The lounge has a wood-burning fireplace and picture windows that look out on a panoramic view of the river. The intimate bar opens onto a lovely patio with a water view. A wide stairway descends to the dining-room level, then to the indoor swimming pool and a glass-walled function room. From the lower-level terrace a steep path winds through the woods past the tennis court and continues to a secluded rocky beach along the fifteen-mile-wide St. Lawrence River.

La Pinsonnière (which means the house of the singing sparrow) is a member of the prestigious Relais & Chateaux organization. The continuing personal involvement of the owners, Jean and Janine Authier and their daughter Valérie Andrée, is what gives this inn the edge over other top places. You can sense their commitment to excellence at every turn.

The newest deluxe room has a large bay window with window seats overlooking the entrance courtyard. A raised double-faced wood-burning fireplace is visible from the king-size brass bed and the large therapeutic hydromassage whirlpool bathtub. The bath also has a small sauna and shower. In two of the deluxe rooms amenities include a king-size brass bed, wood-burning fireplace, bath with double Jacuzzi and a separate glass shower, and a doorway leading to a large semi-private deck with tables and chairs and a view of the St. Lawrence River.

Accommodations range from the deluxe rooms with fireplaces and double Jacuzzis, to rooms with queen-size canopy beds and a fireplace, to suites (including a duplex) and standard rooms, all of which are spacious. Standard rooms have a queen-size bed, full bath, television, and phone; many have views of the river. Small dogs are permitted in one of the rooms.

The Authiers' private English riding center, which has six horses that guests can ride during the day, is a short drive from the inn.

For breakfast we had pastry and freshly squeezed orange juice, followed by a choice of entrée. The thin crêpes with blueberries and pure maple syrup were far superior to traditional blueberry pancakes. Other choices included a fruit plate with Swiss cheese, grilled bread with melted cheese, eggs with a choice of breakfast meats, or French toast. Breakfast concluded with a light dessert course of French toast or a plain or fruit-filled crêpe.

The restaurant is an impressive sight: widely spaced tables with armchairs, picture windows overlooking the vast St. Lawrence River, walls decorated with the owners' collection of Québec art, and a wood-burning fireplace. The staff is polished and professional, but not stuffy. The cuisine is classical, with more herbs and less cream than is traditional in French cooking.

For appetizers at dinner we had an intensely flavored soup of fish stock and parsley juice with oysters and scallops and ravioli filled with shrimp and langoustines, served in a lobster broth. For a main course we had three very mild shark filets served on artichoke bottoms and tomatoes. A second choice was a lamb chop placed inside a spicy lamb sausage and molded to resemble a lamb roast. Different vegetables complement each entrée.

Owner Jean Authier has a 10,000-bottle wine cellar that has won a Wine Spectator Award of Excellence, one of only five given in all of Canada. Instead of the regular menu, you can arrange to have the *dégustation* menu of five courses or the gourmand menu of seven courses; for an extra fee, the staff will match each of the courses with a two- or three-ounce glass of wine. Don't pass up the cheese course, as special attention is devoted to the selection and care of the cheeses.

Our favorite dessert was the individual large round puff-pastry apple tart. A chocolate cup filled with chocolate sherbet was also superb. Chocolate-dipped strawberries, candied orange peel, and cookies were presented with coffee.

Twenty-seven rooms, all with private bath. May through October and the holiday season, $250–$340, breakfast, dinner, and gratuities included. Mid-January through April, $230–$325. Closed November through mid-December. Two- and-three-night packages available: nightly seven-course gourmet dinner, whale-watching cruise package, honeymoon package. Dinner served nightly, 6 to 9 P.M.; three-course dinner, $39; six courses

$55. 124 St.-Raphael, Cap-à-l'Aigle, Québec G0T 1B0; (418) 665-4431.

What to Do. La Pinsonnière is ninety miles north of Québec City by car. The drive up the Charlevoix coast to La Pinsonnière features spectacular scenery and views of the St. Lawrence River. In the artists' town of Baie-Saint Paul, eighteen galleries feature excellent Charlevoix and Québec painters. Heading north from the inn, Route 138 to Tadoussac passes through beautiful hilly country. Three-hour whale-watching cruises leave from Baie-Sainte Catherine and Tadoussac from early June to mid-October. Among the whales that feed along the Charlevoix coast are the humpback and the blue whale. From July to mid-September, four- to five-hour cruises leave from Baie-Sainte Catherine and Tadoussac and go up the Saguenay Fjord. This is the southernmost fjord in the world; its sheer rocky cliffs (up to 1,500 feet high) drop down to the river, which has an average depth of 787 feet.

How to Get There. Cap-à-l'Aigle, about ninety miles northeast of Québec City, is on the northern bank of the St. Lawrence River. From Québec City, take Route 138 east all the way to Cap-à-l'Aigle. For a more scenic drive, turn off Route 138 at Baie-St. Paul and follow Route 362. This road will return to Route 138 at La Malbaie, the town just south of Cap-à-l'Aigle.

The Inn at Canoe Point, *Bar Harbor, Maine*

Tucked into a quiet cove on the rocky Maine coast, The Inn at Canoe Point offers spacious rooms, picture windows, wood-burning fireplaces, and gourmet breakfasts. To get there, turn off the main road leading into busy Bar Harbor onto a narrow gravel drive that winds through a stately grove of evergreens.

Dominating the first floor of this century-old Tudor-style home is the ocean room, with floor-to-ceiling windows overlooking Frenchman's Bay. In summer breakfast is served on the wide deck that wraps around the room. In colder weather a favorite spot is the curved sectional sofa set in front of the granite fireplace. Two easy chairs with a pair of binoculars within reach are ideal for armchair birders. Placed about the room are pieces of Lalique crystal from innkeeper Don Johnson's collection, an abundance of plants and flowers, and a dish filled with chocolate candy kisses. Delve into the extensive library upstairs for a good book or a few magazines and you won't want to leave the inn until dinnertime.

The entry-hall living room has a tuned baby grand piano for guests' use, an Italian armoire filled with additional pieces of Lalique, and a wood-burning fieldstone corner fireplace.

The most romantic room is the large Master Suite, with a late-nineteenth-century chaise longue and two easy chairs set by the fireplace. From the queen-size bed, you'll have a wonderful view of the water. A deck with lounge chairs is shared with the adjoining Anchor Room, which is smaller than the Master Suite but is the only room in the inn with a double whirlpool tub.

The secluded third-floor Garret Suite has two separate rooms, one with a king-size bed and the other with a daybed. Three windows situated directly in front of the king-size bed give a clear view of the water. The main attraction of this suite, however, is that you have the entire third floor as your private domain.

For romance on a more moderate budget, pick the smallest room in the house, the Garden Room, which gives the illusion of being the largest. Windows on three sides let you hear and see the ocean and feel as though your toes are practically in the water. The queen-size bed is nestled inside a white wicker railing. Down a step, a sitting area is furnished with a white wicker settee and rocker. Off the sitting area is your own private entrance, which leads directly to the rocky shore.

In the rooms, thick terry robes, a decanter of port (except for the Port-Side Room, where the brown decor coordinates better with a decanter of sherry), and cocktail napkins embossed with the room's name are thoughtful touches.

At breakfast, the combination of good food and a spectacular setting encourages lengthy conversations with other guests. What better way to start the day than with a glass of fresh orange juice followed by fresh fruit, a hot entrée such as Don's spinach quiche (one of the best we've ever had), apple crisp, or cinnamon French toast?

Five rooms, each with private bath. Memorial Day to mid-

October, $115–$195; other times of the year, $85–$140. Full breakfast is included. Because of its proximity to the water, the inn is not appropriate for younger children. No pets. Box 216, Hulls Cove, ME 04644; (207) 288-9511.

Where to Dine. During the season, we suggest George's (7 Stephens Lane; 207-288-4505), the Porcupine Grill (123 Cottage Street; 207-288-3884), and Miguel's Mexican Restaurant (51 Rodick Street; 207-288-5117) in Bar Harbor. The Asticou Inn in Northeast Harbor (207-276-3344) is a more traditional formal restaurant; its Thursday night buffet includes dancing on the terrace to forties swing music. The Jordan Pond House on the loop road in Acadia National Park (207-276-3316) has a pretty setting and is open for lunch, tea, and dinner.

If you don't mind driving thirty to forty-five minutes, we also recommend Le Domaine on Route 1 in Hancock (207-422-3395) and the Blue Hill Inn (Union Street; 207-374-2844) or Jonathan's (Main Street; 207-374-5226) in Blue Hill. For lobster-in-the-rough in picturesque settings away from the tourists, our favorite spots are Tidal Falls Lobster Pound in Hancock (Tidal Falls Road; 207-422-6818) and Oak Point Lobster Pound in Trenton (Oak Point Road; 207-667-8548). If you're here in the winter, spring or fall, we suggest the Cranberry Lodge (207-276-3344) or Redfields, both in Northeast Harbor, and the Carrying Place in Bar Harbor.

What to Do. Hiking, horseback riding, canoeing, and swimming can all be enjoyed in Acadia National Park during the summer. Take the loop road through the National Park to Thunder Hole, Cadillac Mountain (a hike to its summit at dawn is a popular pilgrimage for those who want to be the first on the East Coast to see the sunrise) and to the Jordan Pond House for tea and popovers. In Northeast Harbor stop at the Asticou Azalea Garden—a Japanese strolling garden—and Thuya Lodge and Gardens. Take a side trip to Schoodic Point, about forty miles to the north, where the rugged beauty of the coast and the waves are particularly impressive. In winter the carriage trails are groomed for cross-country skiing, and Echo Lake is cleared for skating.

How to Get There. Bar Harbor is 480 miles from New York City and 280 miles from Boston. Fly into Bangor or take I-95 to Bangor. Then take Route 1A south to Ellsworth and Route 3 south to Bar Harbor. The Inn is located off Route 3, just beyond the entrance to Acadia National Park.

JANE STAUFFER

The Blue Hill Inn, *Blue Hill, Maine*

Opening the front door of this traditional brick and white clapboard 1830s New England village inn on a chilly fall afternoon, seeing the fireplace and the couches invitingly set on either side, and being warmly greeted by innkeepers Mary and Don Hartley, we felt right at home.

New wallpaper, curtains, comforters, upholstery, and many nineteenth-century antiques are tastefully coordinated in the rooms. There is ample common space in which guests can relax. The rooms vary in size from enormous to comfortable. Many have yellow-pine floors original to the house. Three of the rooms have separate sitting areas, and three others have fireplaces. If reading in bed and watching the fire after a delicious dinner fits your image of a romantic New England inn, choose Room 5, a second-floor corner room with a queen-size four-poster cannonball bed. Another favorite is Room 10, a first-floor corner fireplace room about fifteen by eighteen feet with a queen-size bed featuring an antique headboard. This room is particularly cheerful since the wallpaper, Oriental rug, and bedspread are in shades of muted red, peach, and pink. Room 4, the third fireplace room, has a king-size bed and an old-fashioned clawfoot tub.

We like Room 8, the longest room in the inn. It has a king-size bed and windows on three sides overlooking the splendid perennial garden. Room 3, formerly two smaller rooms, has a sitting area at one end. The third-floor room with a sitting area is the only one that can accommodate three people.

At 6 P.M. hors d'oeuvres are served either by the fireplace in the cooler months or in the perennial garden next to the inn. We enjoyed this relaxing hour, as it gave us a chance to meet the other guests and talk further with Mary and Don.

The main dining room, which seats twenty-six, has seventeen windows and a chandelier with two tiers of candles, eight of which are lit for dinner. The tables are set with white linen and additional candles. The small parlor is used for small group dinners, for breakfast, or for dinner when only a few people are staying at the inn. When the room is used for dinner, the ten candles in the Persian chandelier are all lit.

A six-course dinner is served at 7 P.M. The first course is soup, such as chicken with petit chicken omelets, spiced winter squash, chilled mushroom with chive meringue, or lobster or crab bisque. The appetizer could be citrus and scallop salad, smoked salmon with mango coulis, mussels with curry and cilantro, or salad with quail. Sorbet is the third "course." A choice of two or three entrées might include duck with cognac served with glazed prunes and pears, swordfish with smoked bacon and cabbage, rack of lamb with rosemary, steamed Maine lobster, pheasant with wild rice and rhubarb, or beef tenderloin with blackened mustard seed or with porcini mushrooms. The salad follows the entrée; watercress and walnut salad or fresh greens with balsamic vinaigrette are often served. A single dessert is offered each night. Previous desserts have included strawberry Napoléon, coffee parfait with coffee-bean sauce, chocolate-walnut genoise, frozen raspberry soufflé, floating island (meringue with chocolate sauce), and cheesecake with Maine blueberries.

Breakfast includes freshly squeezed orange juice, muffins, and cereal plus a choice of four or five entrées. You could have the gratiné of citrus fruits and berries served with crème Anglaise; scrambled eggs with chives and smoked bacon served in a puff pastry shell; amaretto French toast with warm maple syrup, walnuts, and currants; a layered herb omelet with avocado and smoked salmon; or traditional blueberry pancakes.

Special events at the inn include vintner dinners and cooking classes.

Eleven rooms, all with private bath, three with fireplaces. July through mid-October, $150–$160 (breakfast and dinner for two included) or $120–$130 (breakfast included). Holidays and Thursday through Saturday other times of the year, $120–$140, breakfast and dinner for two included. Other nights, $80–$110, breakfast included. 15% service charge is additional. Not recommended for children under 13. No pets. No smoking. Dinner served nightly June through October; Thursday through Saturday in November through May. For outside guests by reservation, $35 per person, plus tax, gratuity, and drinks. Innkeeper's

reception 6 P.M., dinner at 7 P.M. Union Street, Box 403, Blue
Hill, ME 04614; (207) 374-2844.

What to Do.   Communities to visit on the peninsula include
Blue Hill, Castine, Deer Isle, and Stonington, all of which have
many galleries, antique shops, and craft stores. This is a major
crafts area. On Deer Isle, the well-known Haystack Mountain
School of Crafts (207-348-2306) and the Wooden Boat School
(207-359-4651) are open in the summer only; call to find out
visiting hours. In Blue Hill, visit two pottery factories, Row-
antrees (Union Street; 207-374-5535) and Rackliffe (Route 172,
north of Blue Hill; 207-374-2297); the Leighton Gallery on Par-
ker Point Road (207-374-5001), one of the top galleries in Maine;
and the studios of artists who live nearby: Ron Pearson for
jewelry (Old Ferry Road, Deer Isle; 207-348-2535), Bill Mor for
pottery (Reach Road, Deer Isle; 207-348-2822), and Kathy
Woell for handwoven jackets (207-348-6141).

Take a day's sail from Stonington, Castine, or Brooksville;
take the mailboat to Isle au Haut and walk the trails; or hike to
the top of Blue Hill mountain. During the summer, attend the
Kneisel Hall chamber music concerts. The Left Bank Café, a
good choice for lunch, holds weekly concerts throughout the
year (Route 172 north of Blue Hill; 207-374-2201). During the
winter, attend a concert at the Congregational church, take a
sleigh ride, or watch and participate in the weekly contra dancing. Acadia National Park is about an hour's drive north.

How to Get There.   Blue Hill is 460 miles from New York
City and 260 miles from Boston. Take I-95 north to Augusta.
Take Route 3 north to Belfast. Take Route 1 north to Route 15
south. Follow Route 15 south to Blue Hill. The inn is on Union
Street in the middle of town.

JANE STAUFFER

The Keeper's House, *Isle au Haut, Maine*

The Keeper's House is a most unusual inn located on rugged Isle au Haut, a little-known appendage of Acadia National Park in East Penobscot Bay, eight miles from Stonington, Maine. There are no phones and no electricity here; a marine radio is available for emergencies, and gaslights, candles, and hurricane lamps provide illumination. Bathrooms are shared, and one of the little cottages has an outhouse. Access to Isle au Haut is a forty-minute trip by mailboat, which makes a stop at the Keeper's House dock.

But before you tire of reading about the romantic lighting in a bed and breakfast without electricity, let us strongly caution that this is not a romantic hideaway for everyone. The remote nature of the island, and the frontier amenities of the inn itself, are not for those who covet large, luxuriously furnished rooms, extensive gourmet menus, and fine shops nearby. For those, on the other hand, who find contentment in the splendor of thick forests and a pristine shoreline, we cannot recommend the Keeper's House strongly enough. Go and enjoy!

The largest room of the four in the main house is the third-floor Garret Suite, which has a double bed and a small sitting area. One of the inn's two bathrooms is on the third floor. The other three rooms, all with double beds and one with a trundle bed, are on the second floor. The Keeper's Room, the original master bedroom, is popular for its view of the lighthouse and for its woodstove. The Sunrise Room also has a woodstove. The Horizon Room looks westward and has the best view of any room in the main house. The furnishings are purposely kept simple, so as not to detract from the natural surroundings.

There are also two tiny guest cottages on the premises. The Oil House (we think of it as a dollhouse, as it is only about 10 feet square) is furnished with a futon couch that unfolds into a bed, a potbellied stove, dresser, table, and hurricane lamps. Two chairs sit on a tiny deck overlooking the water, and a short path leads through the trees to an outhouse, a pleasant shingled building on a scenic bluff. There is an outdoor solar-heated shower on the beach that's surrounded by a low redwood fence so that you can shower and look at the ocean at the same time. While this is certainly the most primitive accommodation it has a definite appeal, since it is the most private, away from the other buildings.

The Wood Shed Room is located on the second floor of a small barn that's close to the main building. A small wooden staircase with railing and support columns made of gnarled spruce limbs winds up to the room, which has a double bed, a window on one wall that gives a view of the sea, three windows on another wall that overlook the forest, and built-in pine furniture to maximize the small space. Guests staying here share the bathroom on the first floor with the innkeepers, Jeff and Judi Burke, who stay on the first floor.

Before dinner you can hike or just lounge about, sipping wine (we suggest you bring a bottle, as the inn has no liquor license), nibbling hors d'oeuvres, and watching the seals play as the sun casts shadows on the lighthouse. Dinner is served in the dining room and all the guests sit together under the glow of gaslights. The dinner we had, typical of those served here, included cream of broccoli soup; a fresh garden salad with a curry Chablis dressing; fish baked in a mixture of herbs, lemon, tomato, and feta cheese; and a piece of chocolate cake. On Sunday nights Jeff and Judi steam lobsters on the beach, always a favorite event.

After dinner we left for our rooms with a candle. The warm rose light from the working lighthouse played on the white walls of the bedrooms. After breakfast, we hitched a ride to the village in the Burkes' 1950 Willys Jeep (one of five on the island). As the island has no restaurants, Judi packs picnic lunches for her guests.

Open May through October. Four rooms and two cottages, all sharing baths or outhouses, $240.75 for two (includes three meals a day, lodging, and taxes). Additional expenses include the mailboat ($9 per person each way during the summer) and parking in Stonington ($4 per day). The mailboat leaves daily except Sunday from Stonington. All reservations must be made well in advance, as there is no telephone on the island. Two-night stay is required in July and August. Children welcome; $53.50 (including tax) for a third person. No pets. No smoking. Box 26, Isle au Haut, ME 04645; (207) 367-2261 for off-island information and reservations.

What to Do. Thirty-two miles of well-groomed, rarely used national park trails crisscross the island. We enjoyed the 3.8-mile Duck Harbor trail, which winds through a moss-carpeted forest that looks like a natural Japanese bonsai garden; the winds and harsh winters have stunted the trees. We were ecstatic to get within fifty feet of an osprey nest, and we've heard there also is an eagle's nest on the island. The island's village has a one-room schoolhouse, a general store, and the Union Congregational Church. The Burkes have maps of the island and will suggest places to hike and poke around. There are also bicycles at the Keeper's House that guests can rent for $12 a day to explore the fourteen miles of roads on the island.

How to Get There. Stonington is about 480 miles from New York City and about 280 miles from Boston. From Portland, take I-95 north to Augusta. Take Route 3 east to Orland, then Route 15 south to Stonington. Access to Isle au Haut is by mailboat, which leaves from Stonington. The Burkes will send you the mailboat schedule and parking information on request.

JANE STAUFFER

A Little Dream, *Camden, Maine*

We sat on the blue Victorian sofa in the pink-tiled sunroom, sipping a glass of strawberry iced tea and nibbling smoked trout pâté. Everywhere we looked, a vignette of artfully arranged Victoriana appeared: teddy bears, antique dolls, quilts, an old-fashioned wheelbarrow filled with plants, a teapot and cups on a little linen-covered table, piles of hat boxes, a violin propped on the mantle. "I'm a collector of collections," Joanne Ball told us when we asked how she and her husband Billy Fontana, a sculptor, had amassed such an extraordinary collection. The four-foot-tall unicorn, the oversized teddy bears, and our favorite, a nineteenth-century Italian marionette, are part of the couple's international collection of folk-art toys attractively displayed throughout the inn.

The living room has a gas jet fireplace, chintz-covered easy chairs and sofas, ribboned baskets stacked with magazines, a bottle of sherry on a silver tray, and long-stemmed glasses filled with candy. "During the winter the house has a particularly romantic feel," Joanne said. "Then we can really pamper our guests and breakfast can be served as late as the guests wish."

The Master Bedroom has a king-size canopy bed facing a television and VCR. A selection of movies, including *A Room with a View*, *Babette's Feast*, and *Peyton Place* (which was filmed in Camden) is provided, or guests can rent their own. The room also has a chaise longue, a private deck with a table and chairs, and a private bath. The Blue Turret Room, a first-floor room that faces Route 1 and has a water view in winter, is particularly popular in the colder months since it is the only one with a gas jet fireplace. The room has a queen-size bed, an English walnut mirror-front armoire, and white wicker rockers placed in the bay window. The Yellow Room, the choice for honeymooners on a budget, is a smaller room with a queen-size bed, a small private deck, and a bath that is private but not in the room. The Toy Room houses many of Joanne and Billy's toys, including the tall unicorn rocking horse at the bay window.

Two carriage-house apartments behind the inn are perfect for guests who want more privacy. The front unit is a bright and airy suite. It has a bedroom with a queen-size brass bed, living room, wet bar, and a large deck with a table, four chairs, chaise longue, and great water views in winter. The back unit has a cozy, private feel with a queen-size bed, wet bar, a steep spiral staircase leading to a low-ceilinged loft sitting room, and a tiny balcony overlooking the back garden.

At night a breakfast menu is put outside your door so that you can indicate the time you want breakfast, which variety of gourmet coffee or tea you prefer, and whether you'd like a smoked salmon, Brie and apple, or cheddar cheese and ham omelet. The candlelit table in the dining room is a scene of elaborate Victorian perfection: lacy cloths, stemmed glassware, and a decorative cake plate with the day's sweet bread under a glass dome. The breakfast entrée changes daily but might include fruit crêpes, heart-shaped banana-pecan waffles, smoked trout with vichyssoise sauce and dilled eggs, or lemon ricotta soufflé pancakes served with raspberry sauce.

Five rooms, all with private bath. Memorial Day through October, $95–$139. Other times of the year, $70–$95. Afternoon tea and full breakfast included. Not appropriate for children. No pets. No smoking. 66 High Street (Route 1), Camden, ME 04843; (207) 236-8742.

Where to Dine. In season, Miller's Lobster in Spruce Head is the quintessential lobster-in-the-rough spot. Owned and operated by the Miller family, it's located at the end of a dirt road in a quiet cove (off Route 73 between South Thomaston and St. George; 207-594-7406). For fine dining try Cassoulet in Camden and have one of the country French casseroles such as *pot-au-feu,* ragout, or traditional cassoulet (31 Elm Street; 207-236-6304).

The fashionable Belmont (6 Belmont Avenue; 207-236-8053), is a favorite haunt of the Camden summer community. The cod cakes served with red-pepper mayonnaise and southern cole slaw were excellent. The Blue Angel Café (Bayview Street; 207-236-2583) has live music. On Main Street in the center of town is Cappy's Restaurant and sailors' bar, a local hangout (207-236-2254). The Roseway burger came on rye bread with cheese, peppers, onions, and mushrooms.

What to Do.   During the summer you can hike in Camden Hills State Park or take a windjammer day or overnight cruise. Go out on the *Lively Lady* to learn how to catch lobsters, or rent a kayak for a two-hour harbor tour. Camden has a number of good shops and galleries.

The views at Camden and Rockport harbors or at Owls Head lighthouse are so spectacular that you could easily spend the afternoon just watching the boats come and go. Side trips include the Farnsworth Museum in Rockland, which has a collection of Wyeth paintings, and the nearby Owls Head Transportation Museum to see vintage cars and airplanes, especially on certain weekends when they "come alive." Head north to the Maritime Museum and antique jaunts in Searsport. Head south to the Pemaquid Point lighthouse, one of the most photographed on the coast; there's a museum inside with displays that focus on the Maine fishing industry and lighthouses. Open Memorial Day through October.

Monhegan Island is a great place to walk the trails and visit artists' studios. In winter you can take a romantic sleigh ride or go skiing at the Camden Snow Bowl.

How to Get There.   Take I-95 north to the Route 1 exit just before Brunswick. Follow Route 1 north to Camden. The inn is located on the left side of the road just north of the center of Camden.

Squire Tarbox Inn, *Wiscasset, Maine*

"**W**e want to be known as a country inn at the end of a road to nowhere," Bill and Karen Mitman told us as we sat by one of the inn's wood-burning fireplaces, sampling goat cheese that they make from the milk of their Nubian goats. The inn is located south of Wiscasset on Westport Island, which so far has escaped the attention of developers. That's to the liking of Bill and Karen, whose strong interest in country life led them to this quiet location nine years ago. In addition to the goats, who are the star attractions at the inn, the Mitmans also have a horse, two donkeys, and several chickens.

The inn is a collection of connecting Maine buildings from different centuries. The original 1763 cape house was moved to this location in the 1820s. Original owner Samuel Tarbox added a Federal-style home which the Mitmans have restored. Each of the four large rooms in this building has a wood-burning fireplace. Two have king-size beds, one has a queen-size, and the fourth room has a double and a single bed. The other seven rooms are the barn rooms, four of which open off the casual double-story barn sitting room; the other three have private entrances. We chose room 5, a small, low-ceilinged room in the barn, for the balcony and view of the bird feeders outside our Dutch door. We spied a pair of Baltimore orioles, hummingbirds, and evening grosbeaks. All of the rooms have electric mattresses, great for chilly Maine nights.

The wood stove in the barn's common room was lit early in the morning, making the room a cozy place to peruse a carefully selected collection of books. The front living room features a wood-burning fireplace and a bowl of chocolate chip cookies. Help yourself to a drink at the honor bar, then head out to the newly reconstructed 1820 post and beam barn with two rope swings, or beyond to the goats' sheds, which are kept extremely clean. A 1,000-foot path leads through a wooded area to a salt water inlet where there is a floating dock, a rowboat for guests' use, and a small screened building with two chairs. Stay a few days and you'll soon adjust to the easy rhythm of this idyllic spot.

Dining at this unique farm/inn is a memorable experience, far more than just a delicious dinner by a wood-burning fireplace. It begins with an informal cocktail hour at 6 P.M. that features a sampling of goat cheese made at the inn's small licensed cheese plant. We tried a creamy chèvre with chives and garlic, a tellicherry crottin rolled in cracked pepper, and an aged Caerphilly that had a smooth texture and a mellow flavor. Some of the guests gathered round an old-fashioned player piano, some relaxed by the fireplace or the wood stoves in rooms filled with interesting books about Maine, and others strolled down to the water.

The walls in the dining room are old barn boards, and a brick fireplace creates the ambience. We were seated with two other couples who were staying at the inn. A single-entrée four-course dinner is served each evening, although substitutions can be arranged. We started with mushrooms stuffed with spinach and walnuts, followed by a salad of mixed greens with balsamic

vinaigrette dressing. Slightly sweet buns made from goat whey
are a welcome staple on the menu. Our entrée, boneless breast
of chicken stuffed with herbed chèvre encased in a puff pastry
shell, was accompanied by fresh asparagus, honey-glazed baby
carrots, and pan-roasted potatoes. Dessert was an orange-
almond tart with whipped cream. Other nights, the main entrée
might be grilled swordfish, roast pork, broiled scallops, or
poached salmon.

After dessert, diners are invited to the shed to watch the
goats being milked. Chief goat-milker and cheese-maker Karen
Mitman explains the process. On a recent visit, a baby goat not
more than twenty-four hours old seemed to enjoy being the
center of attention.

The breakfast buffet includes fruit, home-baked breads, goat
cheese, and granola.

Open mid-May through October. Eleven rooms, all with private bath. Four rooms with fireplaces. May through July,
$120–$160; August through October, $140–$200, breakfast and
dinner for two included; bed and breakfast, $62–$132. 12%
service charge. Children over 12 welcome; $50 for a third person
in room, including dinner. No pets. Dinner served nightly by
advance reservation only. Cocktails, 6 P.M., dinner, 7 P.M. Prix
fixe, $29. RR 2, Box 620, Wiscasset, ME 04578; (207) 882-
7693.

What to Do.   This rugged rock-strewn shoreline and the
people who call this area of Maine home have been fertile terri-
tory for artists for the past 150 years. You can see their paintings
in the Portland Museum of Art and the Walker Art Building at
Bowdoin College. At the Maine Maritime Museum in Bath you
can see and experience 400 years of Maine's sea-going history.
Drive down to Reid State Park, an idyllic spot for a picnic at
tables on the rocky coast, to watch and listen to the rhythms of

the sea. Or, stop at The Osprey in Robinhood for lunch (at the marina off Route 127; 207-371-2530).

Wiscasset is one of the prettiest villages in Maine, with many houses once owned by sea captains. Take a tour of the Musical Wonder House in Wiscasset to see and hear an incredible collection of music boxes. Wiscasset also has a variety of antique shops, most of which are on Main Street. Drive down and around the many fingers of land that protrude into the ocean. Visit Boothbay Harbor and continue to East Boothbay and Ocean Point, one of the great panoramas of the Maine coastline.

How to Get There.   Take I-95 north to the Route 1 exit just before Brunswick. Follow Route 1 through Bath. Take Route 144 (before you get to Wiscasset) south for eight and a half miles. The inn is located on Route 144 on Westport Island.

View from the Summer Suite

The Inn at Harbor Head, *Cape Porpoise, Maine*

This waterfront cottage overlooks the harbor of Cape Porpoise, two and a half miles from the center of Kennebunkport. Its five rooms were each individually and artistically decorated by innkeeper Joan Sutter with the help of her husband, Dave.

The newest room, and certainly our favorite, is the Summer Suite. Available from mid-May to mid-October only, it has a striking water view. The large bathroom has a double Jacuzzi, peaked ceiling, skylight, and a bidet. The king-size bed is covered with a dramatic black-background flowered chintz bedspread. White wicker furniture adds to the breezy feeling.

The Harbor Suite is decorated with a trompe l'oeil mural painted by Joan. Scenes of the fishing harbor cover the walls of one room and the harbor islands—Green, Vaughns, and Bass—decorate the other room. The queen-size cherry pencil-post bed is draped with a fishnet canopy. The tiny corner bath has a skylight and a long brass shower spigot.

You'll notice a Japanese influence in the small Garden Room, especially the river pebbles next to the walls at the entrance. The room has a four-poster queen-size fishnet canopy bed with a lacy crochet spread and the same glorious view as the Summer Suite. French doors open onto a private deck, set with a table and chairs, that offers a beautiful view of the water.

The Greenery's chintz draperies cover three sides of the room, a cheerful backdrop for the queen-size iron bed and a Jacuzzi with painted tiles designed by Joan. The Ocean Room, the smallest in the inn, has a mahogany queen-size pineapple-post bed and a white armoire and bureau. A collection of books about ocean voyages and shipwreck tales fills the shelves of this room.

Joan's elegant breakfasts, served to the strains of classical or New Age music, always include freshly squeezed orange juice, a fruit course, an entrée, and freshly baked muffins. The fruit course might be broiled bananas, pears poached in cranberry juice served with crème fraîche, or peaches and blueberries in spiced white wine. Typical entrées include French toast stuffed with cream cheese and ricotta and covered with a fruit sauce; sourdough rounds sautéed with chicken, shallots, and a cream sauce; or the Montana Big Sky Special, a combination of grated potatoes, sausage, Monterey jack cheese, and salsa.

As Joan rhapsodized over the beauty of this spot, she told us that many of her guests never leave the grounds during their stay. "They lie in the hammocks, sketch by the water, watch the loons and the seals, and listen to the foghorns and sea gulls," she said.

Five rooms, all with private bath. June through October, $125–$190. Other times of the year, $105–$155. Full breakfast and afternoon hors d'oeuvres included. Children over 12 welcome. Third person in the Harbor Suite, $25 additional. No pets. No smoking. Pier Road, R.R. 2, Box 1180, Kennebunkport, ME 04046; (207) 967-5564.

Where to Dine.   For romantic, elegant dining we suggest The White Barn Inn (Beach Street, Kennebunkport; 207-967-2321). We feel that its food and service are the best in the area. The main room is a two-story restored barn decorated with rakes, decoys, rocking chairs, signs, and other items typically saved by thrifty New Englanders. Entrées include baked, stuffed, steamed, or shelled and sautéed lobster; free-range chicken with a veal and herb stuffing; sirloin steak with a green peppercorn sauce; and rack of lamb.

If you don't want to leave the seclusion of Cape Porpoise, walk down the street to Seascapes, which overlooks the working harbor (207-967-8500). We had an excellent meal of lobster tequila—linguine tossed with lobster, spinach, peppers, and cilantro and flavored with tequila and lime. For lobster-in-the-rough during the summer, visit the traditional Nunan's Lobster Hut, a run-down, much-beloved institution (Route 9; 207-967-4435). We sat at picnic tables in this wonderfully cramped black and red building enjoying our lobsters, steamers, and blueberry pie. Also in Cape Porpoise is Tilly's Shanty, a shack perched on the edge of the water, which is a good lunch stop for fried clams or lobster (Pier Road; 207-967-5015). You can get lobster year-round at The Lobster Pot restaurant on Route 9 in Cape Porpoise (207-967-4607).

What to Do.   Spend a day in Kennebunkport visiting the galleries. Stroll along Parson's Way, a stretch of paths overlooking the Atlantic Ocean, with benches at intervals. When the tide and the wind are up, the endless drama of the sea unfolds before you as waves thunder upon the rocks. Farther along, you'll see cars pulled off the road. Curious visitors with binoculars and cameras are taking pictures of Walker's Point, former president George Bush's summer home.

Rent bicycles from Cape-Able Bike for backroad exploring, or spend the day antiquing along Route 1. The beaches are some of the finest in Maine. This is Maine, however; the water is cold, except for late August and September. Goose Rocks Beach is the closest to Cape Porpoise. Parson's Beach south of Kennebunkport is close to the Rachel Carson Wildlife Refuge, a pleasant place to take a walk and learn about the salt marsh ecosystem. Drive over to Ogunquit, about fifteen miles south of Kennebunkport: see a play at the Ogunquit summer theater and walk the Marginal Way, a mile-long footpath along the cliffs overlooking uninterrupted vistas of the Atlantic Ocean. The discount stores in Freeport are a good option for a rainy day, and L.L. Bean, of course, is a Maine institution.

How to Get There.   Take I-95 north to exit 3, then take Route 35 east, following signs to Kennebunkport. Route 9 intersects with Route 35 at Kennebunkport. Follow Route 9 east about two miles from Kennebunkport to Cape Porpoise. Leave Route 9 where it turns sharp left; go straight ahead one-quarter mile past the Wayfarer Restaurant to the inn on your right.

JANE STAUFFER

The Captain Lord Mansion,
Kennebunkport, Maine

"**We** sell romance," declared Bev Davis who, along with husband Rick Litchfield, owns and operates this distinguished mansion, built in 1812 by a sea captain and situated in Kennebunkport on a hill at the edge of the town green. The moment you step into the high-ceilinged, antiques-filled, Oriental-carpeted common room, you will sense a quiet elegance. The furnishings in the bedrooms are nineteenth-century antiques. To provide comfort for today's travelers, the massive, high four-poster beds have all been "stretched" to accommodate firm king-size and queen-size mattresses. Most of the rooms in the Captain Lord Mansion and all the rooms in the Captain's Hideaway, a separate building, have fireplaces; they use between 6,000 and 8,000 Duraflame logs a year.

The rooms are named after ships that sailed in Captain Lord's fleet. First- and second-floor rooms have nine-and-a-half-foot ceilings, while the third-floor rooms have eight-foot ceilings. The deluxe rooms have small, well-stocked minibars that operate on the honor system; guests in the other rooms help themselves to juices and sodas from the inn's refrigerator, also on the honor system.

Our favorite fireplace room is the expansive first-floor Brig Merchant. It was recently redecorated with Schumacher wallpaper, swag and jabot curtains, and red carpeting. Furnishings include an English dressing table and a massive armoire with a writing desk in the center. The Honduran mahogany high queen-size canopy bed dates from 1830. There are steps on both sides of the bed (a boon to the guest who happens to get up in the middle of the night).

Another favorite is the Lincoln Room on the second floor. This room has an 1820 English four-poster queen-size bed, emerald-green carpeting, window seats, a peach-colored sofa, and a fireplace.

Ship Harvest, on the third floor, has a country look. The room is dominated by a king-size custom-made four-poster bed with a carved headboard. Above the fireplace is a mural scene of Kennebunkport in the 1800s, painted by Frank Handlen. Country decorations include an old cobbler's bench and a roulette wheel from a Maine country fair.

Breakfast is served family style at two long tables in the country kitchen at 8:30 and 9:30 A.M. It includes homemade muffins and fruit breads, orange juice, yogurt, berries, muesli, boiled eggs, and a hot entrée such as apple-cinnamon or blueberry pancakes, French toast, or cheese strata. In the afternoon, a plate of home-baked cookies or cakes along with a kettle of warm Swedish glögg, a punch made here with cranberries, are left in the kitchen.

Travelers desiring a more secluded setting should ask about The Captain's Hideaway, a separate building behind the inn. For the ultimate in romance, reserve the Captain's Room. The huge bathroom has a stall shower and a step-up double Jacuzzi, surrounded by mirrors, which faces a fireplace. There is also a wingback chair in this room. The adjoining bedroom has a queen-size canopy bed and a wood stove.

The Garden Room has a private patio entrance, four-poster queen-size bed, fireplace, and a bath with a small Japanese-style Jacuzzi. The four guests at The Captain's Hideaway are served a full breakfast in that building's dining room. The meal includes a choice of juices; fresh fruit; miniature muffins; sausage, bacon, or ham; and an entrée such as eggs Benedict, cheese strata, or pancakes.

Phoebe's Fantasy is a third building with four rooms, each with a king- or queen-size bed. The common gathering room has a large-screen television, fireplace, and an attractive plush chintz sofa. Guests who are staying at Phoebe's Fantasy are served their breakfast in this building. An advantage of staying in either of the smaller buildings is the opportunity to linger over breakfast since there is only one seating.

The Captain Lord Mansion, sixteen rooms, all with private bath and eleven with fireplaces. May through December, $149–$199; November through April, $99–$159. The Captain's Hideaway, two rooms with private bath, both with fireplaces, $199 and $249. Phoebe's Fantasy, four rooms, all with private bath, same rates as at Captain Lord Mansion. Afternoon tea and full breakfast included. Children over 6 welcome. $25 additional for third person in the room. No pets. Box 800, Kennebunkport, ME 04046; (800) 522-3141 or (207) 967-3141.

Where to Dine. For romantic, elegant dining we suggest The White Barn Inn (Beach Street, Kennebunkport; 207-967-2321). We feel that its food and service are the best in the area. The main room is a two-story restored barn whose walls and second floor are decorated with decoys, rakes, rocking chairs, signs, and other items typically saved by thrifty New Englanders. Entrées include baked, stuffed, steamed, or shelled and sautéed lobster; free-range chicken with veal and herb stuffing; sirloin steak with green peppercorn sauce; and rack of lamb.

Other lunch or dinner choices are Litchfield's in Wells (Route 1; 207-646-5711), Windows on the Water (Chase Hill Road; 207-967-3313), and Mabel's (Ocean Avenue; 207-967-2562) in Kennebunkport, and Seascapes, overlooking the water in nearby Cape Porpoise (207-967-8500). For casual local fare we enjoyed a lobster roll and some fried clams at Tilly's Shanty (Pier Road; 207-967-5015), lobster-in-the-rough during the summer at Nunan's Lobster Hut (Route 9; 207-967-4435) or year-round at The Lobster Pot (Route 9; 207-967-4607).

What to Do. Spend a day in Kennebunkport visiting the galleries. Stroll along Parson's Way, a stretch with benches and paths overlooking the Atlantic Ocean. When the tide and the wind are up, the endless drama of the sea unfolds before you as waves thunder upon the rocks. Farther along, you'll see cars pulled off the road. Curious visitors with binoculars and cameras are taking pictures of Walker's Point, former president George Bush's summer home.

Rent bicycles from Cape-Able Bike for back road exploring. Spend the day antiquing along Route 1. Kennebunk Beach is the closest, but we particularly like Goose Rocks Beach and Parson's Beach, some of the finest in Maine. (Do remember this is Maine; the water is cold except for late August and September.) Drive about fifteen miles south to Ogunquit, see a play at the Ogunquit summer theater, and walk the Marginal Way, a mile-long footpath along the cliffs overlooking uninterrupted vistas of the Atlantic Ocean. Shopping enthusiasts will want to visit L.L. Bean and the discount stores in Freeport.

How to Get There. Take the Maine Turnpike I-95 north to exit 3. Take Route 35 east to Kennebunk. Take Route 9 across the bridge over Kennebunk River and turn right onto Ocean Avenue. The inn is a few blocks down the street on your left.

Nestlenook Farm, *Jackson Village, New Hampshire*

This deluxe Victorian bed and breakfast owned by Robert and Nancy Cyr is situated on sixty-five acres overlooking formal gardens, a heated swimming pool, a Victorian chapel, and a three-acre stocked trout pond.

The inn's setting evokes images created by fairy tales. Guests can enjoy the luxury of vast private space whether they visit in the summer or winter. Amenities include an open porch with a swing; an enclosed front porch with wicker furniture covered with chintz pillows; two living rooms, one with a fireplace; and a pub. In winter guests become part of Currier and Ives scenes complete with horse-drawn sleigh rides, ice skating on the pond, and hot chocolate and cookies in front of the fireplace in the massive enclosed gazebo. In summer go horseback riding, spend some time in the hammocks by the swimming pool that has swim jets (to create a current), and relax on the powerful electric massage bed. On a rainy day or in the evening, head to the basement recreation room where there is a billiard table, dart board, and a state-of-the-art surround-sound video system.

Nothing has been spared to make Nestlenook a showcase. It is lavishly decorated with coordinated designer fabrics and furnished with high-quality antiques. The dining room has a Victorian bird cage with chirping love birds inside. All of the rooms have Jacuzzis; five are double Jacuzzis.

On the third-floor the ultra-spacious three-room Murdoch Suite is our favorite accommodation, with a bath as big as a bedroom. You can soak in the double Jacuzzi and view the grounds through multipaned windows. The sitting room has a daybed and two easy chairs; a separate bedroom has a queen-size bed. The rooms are named for prominent Jackson artists who supplied the original art on the walls. We stayed in the Horace Burdick Suite, which has a queen-size bed, a separate sitting room with a daybed, and a large bath with a double Jacuzzi. The king-size bed in the William Paskell Room faces the wood-burning fireplace, making this room a top choice for the winter.

Guests have access to a full kitchen. Wine and cheese are served in the afternoon, and in the evening you can munch fresh popcorn while you view movies on videotape. Breakfast includes juice, muffins, fresh fruit, and an entrée such as Belgian waffles with whipped cream and fresh fruit topping, cinnamon French toast, or a vegetable and cheese frittata.

In order to preserve the privacy of the guests, a tour of the first-floor common rooms and grounds is given daily at 2 P.M. only.

Seven rooms and suites, all with private bath. Summer and winter weekends, $175–$250, midweek, $145–$215; spring and late fall, $125–$195. Full breakfast, hors d'oeuvres, and snacks included. Sleigh rides, mountain bikes, Nordic skiing, ice skating, row boats, and fishing also included. 10% service charge. Children over 12 welcome, 30% additional. No pets. No smoking. Dinsmore Road, Jackson Village, NH 03846; (800) 659-9443 or (603) 383-8071.

Where to Dine. On Saturday nights, Nestlenook's horse-drawn trolley transports inn guests to restaurants in Jackson and returns later to bring them back to the inn. At the Wildcat Tavern (603-383-4245), an old rambling building with an atmospheric pub, try "the cholesterol killer" lobster Benedict—sautéed lobster meat on an English muffin topped with poached eggs and smothered with hollandaise sauce. The "extravaganza," one of the specials, is a large plate of shrimp, lobster, and scallops sautéed with garlic, green peppers, mushrooms, and tomatoes served over a wild rice mixture.

At the more casual Thompson House Eatery (603-383-9341), the chicken San Remo—a mound of sautéed chicken, sweet peppers, onions, eggplant, and sundried tomatoes—as well as the meat loaf Parmigiana, amply take care of hefty appetites. Large portions of aged sirloin steak, barbecued ribs, and prime rib pack in the crowds at the Red Parka Pub, a popular hangout that's approaching its twentieth anniversary (Route 302, Glen; 603-383-4344).

What to Do. In the summer you can go swimming or horseback riding at Nestlenook and use the tennis courts at Nordic Village. Visit the top of Mount Washington by the auto road, the cog railroad, or on foot. Pack a picnic lunch and take a hike. We liked the easy hike to Zealand Hut (three hours round-trip); you can eat lunch by beautiful falls and see what a typical Appalachian Mountain Club hut looks like. For a 360-degree view, hike to the top of Kearsage Mountain (five hours round-trip). Another option is the drive to Dixville Notch with lunch at The Balsams. In winter, Nestlenook provides the equipment for its guests to go ice skating or cross-country skiing on the property. Take a romantic champagne sleigh ride in an Austrian sleigh; then go to the indoor swimming pool and hot tub at Nordic Village. There is an extensive system of cross-country trails around Jackson. Downhill ski areas nearby include Wildcat, Black Mountain, and Attitash. If you are the type to "shop till you drop," head to the five-mile strip of North Conway discount stores.

How to Get There.   From Boston, take I-95 north to the Spaulding Turnpike (just before Portsmouth, New Hampshire). Follow Route 16 north to Jackson. From Hartford, take I-86 to the Massachusetts Turnpike (I-90). Exit the turnpike at I-290, which cuts through Worcester, Massachusetts, to I-495 north. Take I-495 north to I-95, just south of the New Hampshire border. Follow I-95 north to Portsmouth. Take the Spaulding Turnpike, also called Route 4, north to Rochester, New Hampshire, then follow Route 16 to Jackson. Turn right at the covered bridge in Jackson. The inn is on your right.

JANE STAUFFER

Rabbit Hill Inn, *Lower Waterford, Vermont*

Tucked into a Vermont hillside near the Connecticut River is Lower Waterford, a thoroughly traditional New England village. The steepled church, stamp-size post office, library, and eighteenth-century houses all are painted white with dark green shutters. Within this storybook setting you'll find the utterly romantic Rabbit Hill Inn.

Arriving in time for tea, which is served from 2 to 6 P.M., the hospitality starts with a personal greeting from innkeepers John and Maureen Magee, their son Matthew, or their assistant Jackie. In winter you will find mulled cider, venison stew, or chili warming in the black kettle that hangs over the hearth in the tavern; in warm weather, sample homemade cookies and iced tea made from red clover, the state flower.

Choosing among the twenty rooms is difficult. Here are some of our favorites: The Loft, the largest room in the inn, has its own private staircase. Special features include a cathedral ceiling, hand-hewn beams, an eight-foot Palladian window, king-size canopy bed, fireplace with a couch and two rocking chairs, and a deck at the back of the inn. The bath has a double whirlpool and a separate shower.

The Nest is a suite on the third floor with a wrought-iron queen-size canopy bed that faces the fireplace, a sun deck, a large dressing room with a chaise longue and mirrored vanity, and a bath with a double whirlpool tub and separate shower.

The Tavern Secret has a king-size fishnet canopy bed, a fireplace, a bookcase wall, a large bath with a double whirlpool and a separate shower, and a secret door.

The spacious third-floor Cummings Suite has a living room with a fireplace, bedroom, and a large private screened porch with a view of the White Mountains.

The oversized Music Chamber suite is equipped with a working pump organ, sheet music of the period, Victrola, a collection of 78s, and a fainting couch, along with a king-size bed and a fireplace.

In Victoria's Chamber a king-size bed is framed with a blue demi-canopy. There is a fireplace, a clothes tree hung with Victorian children's clothing, a Victorian couch, the latest issue of *Victoria* magazine (ordered just for this room), and a letter from the 1890s.

The Top of the Tavern Suite, on the top floor of the Tavern building, has a large bedroom with a sitting area, a queen-size four-poster bed and a fireplace, as well as a dressing room with a vanity, daybed, and a collection of Victorian wardrobe accessories.

Prior to dinner you will find John tending bar and conversing with guests in the tavern, which has a fireplace, couches, and easy chairs, or in the adjoining Irish pub, a separate room with hand-crafted tables and chairs. During dinner, Maureen, an accomplished flutist, occasionally provides background music.

Chef Russell Stannard prepares an inventive menu that changes every two months. We started with delicately flavored shrimp and corn pancakes with garlic-scallion butter and roasted peppers. A taste of cranberry sorbet in champagne followed the Caesar salad. Five to seven entrées are prepared each evening. The most creative and delicate entrée we had included three large sea scallops with their roe still attached, each cooked a different way (steamed, grilled, and sautéed) and each served with a different sauce (basil-cashew pesto, carrot ginger, and red pepper), accompanied by ginger linguine and baby vegetables. Grilled rounds of beef tenderloin seasoned with a Moroccan spice mixture and a spicy peanut sauce garnished with melon and jicama relish came with fluted whipped sweet potatoes flavored with lemon and nutmeg. To top it all off, a divine frozen chocolate mousse had layers of mocha, white chocolate, and dark chocolate with hot fudge and whipped cream.

"Rabbity" touches are discreetly present in the butter molds, napkin rings, and porcelain table decorations. It is this attention to detail that sets Rabbit Hill apart from many other inns.

After an excellent evening meal, return to your room to find it lit by the glow of a candle, soft music playing, the bed turned down with flower petals strewn on the sheets, and a one-of-a-kind "Do Not Disturb" sign: a lacy heart-shaped pillow, the Magees' gift to you.

Rise in the morning to a generous breakfast: juice, muffins or other sweet bread, homemade granola, a fruit course, and a choice of two entrées. We had souffléed French toast with heart-shaped molds of butter and Vermont maple syrup.

Twenty rooms and suites, each with private bath, $149–$219. Fireplace rooms (gas-burning) and suites, $189–$219. Breakfast, afternoon tea, and dinner for two included. 15% gratuity added to all charges. Children over 12 welcome. Third person in room, $65 additional. One wheelchair-accessible room is available. No pets. No smoking. Imaginative picnic lunches can be ordered, $16–$25. Lower Waterford, VT 05848; (800) 76-BUNNY or (802) 748-5168.

Special Theme Weekends at Rabbit Hill

Valentine's Day weekend: Victorian valentines, fresh flowers on your pillow, unusual desserts for two, and much more.

St. Patrick's Day and Halloween: Mystery weekends.

Thanksgiving: Fireplace cookery in the pub.

Christmas: A three-day event includes making tree ornaments and decorating the tree, sleigh rides, fireplace cookery, tobogganing, a candlelight church service, decorated "surprise theme" dining room, and handmade gift.

What to Do. The inn has a swimming pond, gazebo, and hiking trails. Backroading, antiquing, cross-country skiing, downhill skiing, and canoeing are all available in the area; for golfers, the inn has a membership at a nearby club. Visit the St. Johnsbury Athenaeum's art gallery to see the 10-by-15-foot *The Domes of the Yosemite* by Albert Bierstadt and other paintings displayed at the gallery at the back of the library. Take a driving tour of the White Mountains in New Hampshire. If it's a clear day, drive to the top of Mount Washington or take the cog railway to the summit. Drive through Franconia Notch, walk through the Flume, and take the tramway up Cannon Mountain. Stop at the Appalachian Mountain Club at Pinkham Notch for detailed hiking information and maps.

How to Get There. From Boston, take I-93 north to exit 44, then north two miles on Route 18. From Hartford, take I-91 north to exit 19, then I-93 south. Take exit 1 and follow Route 18 seven miles south to the inn.

JANE STAUFFER

Stowehof Inn, *Stowe, Vermont*

A complete equestrian program, a tennis pro in residence during July and August, close proximity to skiing in the winter and hiking in the summer, and utterly romantic sleigh rides for two make Stowehof an ideal romantic getaway for travelers who prefer a physically active vacation.

The architecture of the building is distinctive, with large branching maple trees used as posts to hold up the entrance portico. The back of the building, shaped like the prow of a ship, looks out onto the swimming pool and classic Vermont picture-book mountain scenery. Grass and wildflowers grow on one of the roofs. Large maple trees also serve as support columns in the spacious main floor lounge, which features a sunken stone fireplace and comfortable seating that overlooks the seasonal changes of the Vermont landscape. The Covered Bridge Room has a pool table, Ping-Pong table, and a large-screen television. Other public spaces in this upscale mountain lodge include a library, a tap room that serves up lighter meals and evening entertainment, and a lounge.

The best guest rooms are the five flagship rooms and the four rooms with fireplaces, all of which were recently redecorated. The flagship guest rooms, located at the point of the prow, offer spectacular views. Room 44 is our favorite. This light-filled corner room has a king-size bed and a feminine Victorian feel with a rose-colored cathedral ceiling, pink floral wallpaper, and white carpeting. Room 43, across the hall, has darker-colored Victorian floral print wallpaper with a coordinating print on the cathedral ceiling. This room also has a king-size bed and the same spectacular view as room 44, but you need to step out on the balcony to get the full impact of the landscape. The baths have black marble tiles on the floor. Our pick of the other flagship rooms are in the following order, based on their views: room 45 has a king-size bed and a full view of Mount Mansfield; rooms 46 and 42 each have queen-size beds.

The two best fireplace rooms, each with spectacular views, are room 29, a second-floor room with slightly better view, and room 18, which is directly underneath room 29 and has a more masculine decor. Each has a king-size bed that faces the fireplace, along with an easy chair and kitchenette.

For a more economical choice, we like rooms 36 and 35, both smaller standard rooms, because they are directly underneath rooms 44 and 43, the rooms at the prow of the ship. All rooms have a private patio or a balcony.

The Peterson Brook Farm, a working farm up the road from Stowehof, is owned by the inn. The four newly decorated Barn-hof rooms have an informal European country look. Each has twin beds covered with duvets. At the end of the hall there is a casual lounge area with a fireplace, a large deck, and a kitchen-ette. Some of the rooms have spectacular views, but because the ambiance is less luxurious we do not suggest the lower-priced rooms for a romantic getaway.

In summer, the large floor-to-ceiling windows in the dining room have a view of the lighted pool and landscaped grounds. In winter, you can listen to the sleigh bells and see the twinkle of the lanterns on the antique, sporty Albany Cutter sleigh as it glides across the meadow. On weekends, a pianist plays the Steinway baby grand. What could be more romantic?

The menu, which changes monthly, features basic regional American cooking with an emphasis on local ingredients. The classic Caesar salad has a rich, creamy dressing. A salad of baby lettuce was served with slices of seared foie gras. Hearty soups included lentil and cream of mushroom. A popular creative entrée is salmon roulade, filets layered with salmon mousse which are rolled and sliced. Rack of Vermont lamb, a specialty, and pork loin en croute are both carved tableside. Other entrées included roast quail with a wild rice stuffing, venison breast stuffed with minced homemade sausage, and chicken breast stuffed with broccoli and Vermont cheddar cheese.

The inn is known for its desserts; they are presented on a buffet table in the living room during the busier times of the year. On a winter night it is particularly enjoyable to finish your meal by the fire in the adjoining lounge. We had the apple blueberry pie with a flaky phyllo crust and the apple plum nut pie.

The informal tap room serves lighter meals. In the summer, dining is on the outdoor terrace. The menu includes French onion soup, chicken pot pie, grilled fish, petite sirloin, and pasta dishes.

Guests choose from a full breakfast menu. Start with freshly squeezed orange juice or fresh fruit. Continue with an entrée, which might be grilled homemade cinnamon raisin bread dipped in custard and served with maple syrup; smoked salmon omelet with crème fraîche; scrambled eggs served in puff pastry with mushroom sauce; puff pancakes; a made-to-order omelet; or a fresh fruit and cheese plate.

Forty-six rooms in the inn and four farmhouse rooms, all with private bath, summer and winter season, $128–$188, breakfast included; $180–$240, breakfast and dinner for two included. Weekends in late spring and fall, $135–$145, breakfast and dinner for two included. Lower rates midweek. Packages available. Children welcome; under 4 free, over 4, $35 additional. No pets. 15% gratuity is additional. Dinner in main dining room, 6 to 9 P.M., entrées, $16–$20. Tap room open 5 to 10 P.M. in high season. Box 1108, Edson Hill Road, Stowe, VT 05672; (800) 932-7136 or (802) 253-9722.

What to Do.   In the winter, Mount Mansfield in Stowe has downhill and cross-country skiing. Take a sleigh ride for two in an antique Albany Cutter sleigh. In the summer, you can drive to the top of Mount Mansfield and hike the ridge trail, which offers spectacular views on both sides of the mountain. Hike to Moss Glen Falls, Bingham Falls, or Sterling Falls Gorge. Walk or bike the five-mile asphalt Stowe Recreation Path.

The inn has four tennis courts (lessons are available) as well as horseback riding. A side trip to the forty-five-acre Shelburne Museum (an hour away) to see the 200,000-piece collection of Americana or a backroads drive through the winding, steep Smuggler's Notch are good activities for the summer. At any time of the year you can take the thirty-minute tour of the Ben and Jerry ice-cream factory in nearby Waterbury, where you can sample several of the thirty-four flavors such as Coffee Heath Bar Crunch and Cherry Garcia.

How to Get There.   From New York, take I-91 north to I-89. At Waterbury, Vermont, take Route 100 north to Stowe, then Route 108 north toward Mount Mansfield. Turn right at Edson Hill Road. From Boston, take I-89 to Route 100.

JANE STAUFFER

Jackson House, *Woodstock, Vermont*

The copper roof gleams in the sunlight; the white picket fence is freshly painted; the lamp post is topped by an authentic gaslight; a newly installed moon bridge arches over the stream; and the last and most sumptuous of the eleven rooms is now complete. Since 1983 owners Jack Foster and Bruce McIlveen have been painstakingly restoring and furnishing this museum-quality property.

This inn is not for everyone. Because the furnishings are some of the finest you'll ever see, there are a few rules of the house; guests must remove their shoes indoors during the winter and are asked not to lie on the expensive bedspreads. Don't be put off by the formal trappings, however. Jack and Bruce are warm, otherwise easy-going innkeepers.

A lumber merchant built the house in 1890 using the finest craftsmen and woods available, which explains the floors of oak, cherry, and walnut, as well as the polished cherrywood staircase, all maintained in superb condition.

The parlor, library, and dining room are furnished with wing-back chairs, Sheraton sofas, Chinese porcelains, French-cut crystal, and a 1690 restored English marquetry longcase clock that chimes the hours. A Jacobean gateleg table was rescued from an English pub.

The recently completed Regency Suite is decorated with country antiques and has a slightly more informal decor than the rest of the inn. The cathedral-ceiling living room with exposed rafters includes a wood-burning fireplace, the only one at the inn. There is a full kitchen, a dining room, a den with an entertainment center, small outdoor deck with a barbecue, and a bedroom with a four-poster mahogany queen-size canopy bed. Breakfast is delivered to the suite.

The two sumptuous suites on the third floor of the inn have French doors that open onto a deck overlooking the grounds. Nicholas I has a queen-size cherrywood bed, a burgundy leather sofa, and antique Chinese porcelains. The bathroom and shower have Italian marble on the floor and walls. The second suite, Francesca, is the most lavish of all. It, too, has a queen-size bed and is furnished with antique bureaus and tables, an Italian chandelier, a Japanese lacquered wedding box, and a Japanese teak chest. The bathroom is lined with Italian marble.

The Josephine Tasher Bonaparte Room on the first floor boasts a formal Empire-style mahogany double-sleigh bed with brass adornments, a tufted-leather chair, and gold jabot draperies. The Mary Todd Lincoln Room on the second floor is particularly romantic, with a high-backed Victorian double bed, marble-topped tables, a tufted-velvet Victorian barrel-backed chair, and a Victorian rocker. The Schumacher/Waverly wallpaper and fabrics are authentic to each period room, and every bedroom has a Casablanca paddle fan.

An innkeepers' reception is held each evening at 6 P.M. Complimentary champagne or white wine is served, along with assorted hot and cold hors d'oeuvres. A harpist plays on Saturday night. We sampled caviar, pâté, Swedish meatballs, carpaccio, and hot cheese puffs on our visit. If you are planning to have a full dinner afterward, you'll need to use restraint. When we returned to our room after dinner we found our bed turned down and a little box of Lake Champlain truffles (made in Vermont) on the pillows.

Breakfast, served from 7:30 to 9:30 A.M., is a sumptuous repast served at one large table. We had a choice of bananas served with schlag (whipped cream) or a piece of honeydew with kiwi and grapes; fresh orange juice; a Santa Fe omelet with sun-dried tomatoes, pesto, and cheese; sausage; homemade pecan muffins and scones—all of it delicious. Another of Jack's specialties is a dilled biscuit topped with smoked salmon, poached egg, and hollandaise sauce. After breakfast you can relax in the hammock out back or, for the more energetic, rent bicycles for a ride through Woodstock.

Nine rooms and three suites, each with private bath. Rooms, $125–$136; suites, $175–$225. Early evening hors d'oeuvres, champagne, and wine as well as a full breakfast included. Children over 14 welcome. Rooms are double occupancy only. No smoking. No pets. Two-night minimum stay on weekends and certain holidays. Located one and a half miles west of Woodstock village. Route 4 West, Woodstock, VT 05091; (802) 457-2065.

Where to Dine.   The four-star Hemingway's, about a fifteen-minute drive from the inn (Route 4, Killington; 802-422-3886), was named one of the twenty-five best restaurants in the United States by *Food & Wine* magazine in 1992. For lunch, visit the Simon Pearce Restaurant (802-295-1470), located in a restored mill along the Ottauquechee River in Quechee. In warm weather we like to sit outside on the deck overlooking the waterfall.

What to Do. The historic character of Woodstock has been lovingly preserved. Its classic green is surrounded by examples of Georgian and Federal architecture, and the Ottauquechee River and Kedron Brook flow through the city. Strict laws regulate new development. Utility lines are buried underground. Much of the surrounding hillside is permanently protected from development. For daily and weekly events in Woodstock check the "town crier" blackboard located at the corner of Elm and Central streets. Visit the Billings Farm Museum, where you can trace the daily life of a Vermont family hill farm in 1890. Visit the Simon Pearce Glass Mill, in a spectacular location (above) where you can watch glassblowers and potters at work using power from a modern water-driven turbine. In winter there is skiing at Suicide Six outside Woodstock, or at Killington. There's also a cross-country ski touring center and golf course at the Woodstock Inn.

How to Get There. From New York City take I-95 north to I-91. Take Route 12 to Route 4 west to Woodstock. From Boston take I-89, then west on Route 4 to Woodstock. The inn is located on Route 4, 1.5 miles west of Woodstock.

JANE STAUFFER

Cornucopia of Dorset, *Dorset, Vermont*

You will be pampered to perfection at this intimate nineteenth-century white clapboard bed and breakfast located in the center of Dorset. After innkeeper Bill Ley showed us to our room, we went downstairs for a cup of tea and cookies. His wife Linda arrived with two flutes of champagne, her way of welcoming each guest. Kitt, a well-trained pure-bred Vermont mutt, also welcomed us.

The entire first floor is common space for the guests. A glass-walled sitting area with a pair of white couches, a television, VCR, picture books about Vermont, and a selection of current magazines occupies one end of the dining room. There is a small living room with a fireplace and sitting area. The library has a backgammon table and easy chairs. The terrace is set with Adirondack chairs and overlooks the manicured, intensely culti-vated narrow yard and the cottage.

The attention to detail is not limited to the decor. Bill or Linda will make dinner reservations for you and then leave a written confirmation and a copy of the menu in your room. After dinner we found our bed turned down, an oil lamp burning, a piece of Mother Myrick's buttercrunch candy or a Steininger's truffle on our pillow, the morning breakfast menu, and a tray with brandy in the hall. If you stay in the main house, you can have a pot of coffee or tea served in Royal Doulton china brought up to your room before breakfast.

All the rooms have down comforters in winter and colorful quilts in warmer months. Each room also has a notebook filled with information about the inn, the innkeepers, the local restaurants, the history of the area, and some things to do. The rooms are named after local mountains. We stayed in The Scallop, a corner room with floor-to-ceiling windows, a queen-size canopy bed, and a wood-burning fireplace. Dorset Hill, with a four-poster king-size bed, and Green Peak, a long, spacious room with a four-poster queen-size bed, both look out on the gardens.

For a romantic getaway, stay in Owl's Head, a private cottage located behind the inn. The first-floor living room has a cathedral ceiling, wide-board pine floors, a couch and easy chair facing a brick fireplace. A full kitchen, an outdoor deck with chairs, and the bath also are on the first floor. From the sleeping loft, which has a queen-size bed and two skylights, you can look down into the living room.

The Cornucopia's large breakfast room has an exquisite 18-by-25-foot Oriental rug and French doors that open onto the terrace and garden. Breakfast includes freshly squeezed juice, a fruit salad, and an entrée such as a baked puff pancake served with fresh fruit and warm maple syrup or rum raisin French toast. At breakfast we were entertained by a flock of evening grosbeaks gathered at the window bird feeders.

Four rooms and one cottage suite, each with private bath. Weekends, rooms $100–$130, cottage, $175. Midweek, rooms $90–$110, cottage $155. 10% service charge. Inquire about seasonal specials such as dinner for two, theater or alpine-skiing tickets. Full breakfast included. Air-conditioned. Not appropriate for children. No pets. No smoking. Located on Route 30, Dorset, VT 05251; (802) 867-5751.

Where to Dine. Walk next door to Barrows House (802-867-4455) and try the Maine crabcakes, a house specialty prepared with Old Bay seasoning or salmon stuffed with sun-dried tomatoes, pine nuts, basil, and cream cheese.

Go over Dorset Hill to East Dorset and have an elegant dinner at Chantecleer (Route 7A; 802-362-1616), the best restaurant in this area. Try an appetizer of risotto with mushrooms and sausage, a Caesar salad prepared tableside, or potato pancakes served with a thick crabmeat and lime-butter sauce. The cheese fondue makes a fun meal, and the rack of lamb is carved tableside.

The tavern at the venerable old Dorset Inn (Route 30; 802-867-5500) is one of the gathering spots and watering holes favored by the locals. Drive about 15 miles southwest to Steininger's in Salem, New York, for lunch (Main Street; 518-854-3830). Try a bowl of the homemade soup and a cup of cappuccino. The chocolates are made in the finest European tradition.

What to Do. Walk around Dorset, an idyllic Vermont village. The buildings are white with black or dark green shutters. Peltier's General Store was built in 1817. A few miles down the road is Williams Department Store, an old-fashioned "no frills" store that's been owned by the same family for 100 years. Notice the marble sidewalks and the marble church. Dorset is the site of the first marble quarry on the North American continent. The stone for the New York Public Library came from one of the quarries, which now is a favorite swimming hole.

Route 30 going north out of Dorset runs through the Mettowee Valley for seventeen miles. This is picture-perfect rural Vermont scenery—a valley of dairy and sheep farms, farmhouses, silos, and tillable land. Visit Hildene, the home of Robert Todd Lincoln. Go canoeing or fishing on the Battenkill River, hike on the Appalachian Trail, or play golf on the newly built Glen Eagles course at the Equinox Hotel. Shoppers head to the designer discount stores in Manchester: Anne Klein, Cole-Haan, Polo/Ralph Lauren, Donna Karan, Hickey Freeman, Coach Leatherware, Joan and David, Brooks Brothers, and many more.

How to Get There. From New York City take I-87 to I-787 to Troy. Head east on New York State Route 7 (which becomes Route 9 in Vermont) to Bennington. Take U.S. Route 7 north to Manchester and Route 30 to Dorset. From Hartford, take I-91 north to Brattleboro, then Route 30 west to Manchester Center. Continue six miles to Dorset. From Boston, take the Massachusetts Turnpike west to I-91 north.

1811 House, *Manchester Village, Vermont*

An inn is far more than the sum of its details. You'll know that this inn is in a class by itself as soon as you walk through the door. The original structure was built in the 1770s and has been operated as an inn since 1811. The Victorian porches that were added later have been taken away, excessive molding recently was removed, and modern windowpanes were replaced with old handmade glass. Today the house is a showcase for an extensive collection of English and American antiques, prints, and Oriental rugs that the previous owners accumulated. Innkeepers Marnie and Bruce Duff purchased the inn along with almost all of the furnishings in July 1990. Since then they have greatly expanded the gardens and have fully air-conditioned the buildings.

In the wood-paneled foyer there is a woodcut of the current 1811 House. Beyond is a little English pub called a "snug." High chairs are placed around the polished wood bar; the dark wood tables by the windows are rubbed to a shine; a fireplace, Windsor chairs, and a regulation dart board add to the cozy atmosphere. Marnie and Bruce have put their Scottish coat of arms above the bar. The glasses are Waterford and the liquor selection includes Bruce's collection of single-malt scotch whiskeys. When the inn isn't busy, the bar operates on the honor system. Most evenings it's open to the public for a few hours.

One feature of the 1811 House that we found particularly appealing was the variety of common rooms available to guests. A library and a living room have a working fireplace each. The common rooms have literature about area attractions and de-canters of sherry and port set out for guests. A basement game room made atmospheric with low overhead lamps has both table tennis and a regulation billiard table. The formal dining room, with another fireplace and three separate tables, is a great place for a bridge tournament.

The most romantic rooms are the six with fireplaces and the one with a private balcony. Three of these are located in a newly reconstructed cottage next to the main inn. Our favorite cottage room takes up the entire second floor and has a peaked ceiling. The fireplace is in full view of the king-size bed and the two enormous leather chairs. On the first floor are two additional rooms, each with king-size canopy beds, easy chairs, Oriental rugs, and large modern baths.

In the main inn, the fireplace rooms include the suite on the first floor, with a king-size four-poster, and the two rooms on the second floor, each with queen-size canopy beds. All the rooms have Oriental rugs and reading chairs. The baths in the main inn are not as large as those in the cottage, although they do have old-fashioned clawfoot tubs. If you are visiting during the warmer months ask for the Robinson Room; its king-size bed faces glass doors that open onto a private balcony. The balcony view of the landscaped grounds, pond, and Green Mountains is positively breathtaking. The marble enclosure around the clawfoot tub also lends an air of individuality to this room.

A full breakfast is served from 8 to 9:30 A.M. The choice is yours whether to have it in the snug or in the more formal dining room. Breakfast includes fresh orange or grapefruit juice, fresh fruit, and a different entrée each day. On Saturday it's an English-style breakfast of fried eggs, scones, bacon, grilled tomatoes, apples, and mushrooms. On Sundays it's eggs Benedict. Other days it might be omelets with fried potatoes and English muffins, or pancakes with maple syrup.

Thirteen rooms and one suite, each with private bath, $110–$180. Full breakfast included. Children over 16 welcome. No pets. Two-night minimum stay on weekends and during the fall foliage season. Located on Route 7A, Box 39, Manchester Village, VT 05254; (800-432-1811) or (802) 362-1811.

Where to Dine. The best restaurant in the area is Chantecleer, which serves traditional French food in a converted barn with a magnificent fieldstone fireplace (Route 7A, East Dorset; 802-362-1616). Other good choices are The Arlington Inn in Arlington (Route 7A; 802-375-6532) and the Barrows House in Dorset (Route 30; 802-867-4455). The Equinox Hotel and the Reluctant Panther are across the street from the 1811 House.

What to Do. Shoppers flock to Manchester and its more than seventy designer outlets and upscale boutiques, including

Orvis, Anne Klein, Ralph Lauren, Coach, Harvé Bernard, Liz
Claiborne, Hickey Freeman, Ellen Tracy, and Brooks Brothers.
Visit Hildene, the home of Robert Todd Lincoln; attend the
Orvis fly-fishing or shooting school; canoe on the Battenkill River
or golf on the new Glen Eagles course at the Equinox; drive
over the Green Mountains on the Kelly Stand Road. See a
performance at the Dorset or Weston Playhouse and visit the
antique shops and galleries in the area. The two closest ski
areas are Bromley and Stratton. For cross-country skiing, try
Stratton, Hildene, or Wild Wings.

How to Get There. From New York City, take the New
York State Thruway (I-87) north to I-787 to Troy. Head east on
New York State Route 7, which becomes Route 9 east at the
Vermont-New York border. Continue east on Route 9 to Ben-
nington. Take U.S. Route 7 north to Manchester, then go south
on Route 7A one mile to the inn.

From Hartford, take I-91 north to Brattleboro. Go west on
Route 30 to Manchester. From Boston, take the Massachusetts
Turnpike west to I-91 north.

JANE STAUFFER

Cliffwood Inn, *Lenox, Massachusetts*

Set back from the road on a quiet street of large, elegant homes, two blocks from the center of Lenox, stands Cliffwood Inn. This 1890s mansion, built for a French ambassador during the Gilded Age, is in the grand Stanford White style. The circular drive leads to an impressive portico supported by eight Ionic columns and a heavy carved wooden door framed by decorative mullioned windows.

Outfitting an inn with fine furnishings was no problem for owners Joy and Scottie Farrelly, as they had amassed a sizeable collection of furniture, paintings, Oriental rugs, and accessories during twenty-five years of corporate moves among the capitals of Europe. Over the years they commissioned furniture makers in France, Italy, and Belgium to craft reproductions of museum pieces that would complement the antiques they purchased. They even had an artist copy several of Canaletto's Venetian scenes. The Farrellys also are dealers in Eldred Wheeler Colonial reproduction furniture and use pieces in furnishing the rooms.

Polished inlaid hardwood floors and twelve-foot ceilings distinguish the first floor. In keeping with the magnitude of the house, there's a grand piano in the front hall. Two little bench seats on either side of a small fireplace in the front hall are favorite reading spots. Huge gilded mirrors make the expansive living room, comfortably arranged with sofas and easy chairs, appear extraordinarily large.

In the summer, breakfast is served on the 850-square-foot veranda, which overlooks the pool and landscaped grounds. The dining room is graced by a Venetian chandelier and a 400-year-old sideboard. Except for midweek during the off-season, a copious continental breakfast of fresh fruit (in cool weather, a hot fruit compote or baked apples and crème fraîche), homemade granola, juice, breads, muffins, and croissants is served.

The second-floor sitting area includes a large bookcase filled with art books neatly arranged by country of origin. A major advantage for guests at Cliffwood is Scottie Farrelly's computerized listing of performances by the more than forty different arts groups that call the Berkshires home during the summer months. When you make your reservation, be sure to ask for a listing of events coinciding with your stay.

Six of the seven bedrooms, which are named for ancestors of the Farrellys, have working fireplaces. The Walker Room, one of the largest, has a king-size four-poster bed, a chaise longue, and a fireplace. We were quite taken with the Jacob Gross, Jr., Room, which has a king-size canopy bed, a writing desk, easy chairs, fireplace, and a private balcony. The bath is bright blue and includes a bidet. The Walker/Linton Suite has two rooms. The bedroom includes a queen-size four-poster canopy bed and a chaise longue. In the adjoining room there is a queen-size convertible couch and a fireplace. The newly redone Nathaniel Foote Room on the third floor was made by removing the wall between two smaller rooms. This room, now one of the best, has a queen-size four-poster canopy bed, Oriental rugs, and a fireplace. For those on a budget, some of the lower-priced rooms have fireplaces.

The location of the inn makes it ideally suited for music lovers; not only is Cliffwood in Lenox, but the street the inn is on leads directly to an entrance to Tanglewood that bypasses the usual traffic jams. In addition, the landscaped grounds, the large swimming pool, and the many restaurants and shops nearby make this a getaway where a car is not an absolute necessity. Visitors from abroad may be pleased to know that Joy and Scottie Farrelly speak French, Italian, and Spanish.

Seven rooms, each with private bath, six with fireplaces. July and August, foliage season and holidays, $105–$185; other times of the year, $74–$133. Three-night stay required on weekends during the high season. Copious continental breakfast (except during midweek low season), wine, and hors d'oeuvres included. Children over 13 welcome; $20 additional. No pets. No credit cards. Located off Route 7A in the center of Lenox. 25 Cliffwood Street, Lenox, MA 01240; (413) 637-3330.

Where to Dine.   For the ultimate in palatial surroundings and preparation, head to Wheatleigh for the tasting dinner (West Hawthorne Road; 413-637-0610). The Village Inn (16 Church Street; 413-637-0020) and Church Street Café (69 Church Street; 413-637-2745) are within walking distance of the inn.

What to Do.   For more than fifty years, the Boston Symphony Orchestra at Tanglewood has been, well, instrumental in turning the Berkshire region into one of the great summer cultural destinations in the country. The orchestra performs during July and August at Tanglewood, and first-class chamber music, choral music, theater, and dance are all available nearby. The Norman Rockwell Museum, which houses more than 600 of the artist's paintings and drawings, is located in Stockbridge.

Herman Melville wrote the great American novel *Moby Dick* at Arrowhead, his home, located outside Pittsfield. The Clark Art Institute in Williamstown has an outstanding collection of seventeenth- through nineteenth-century paintings, including works by Gainsborough, Rembrandt, Renoir, Degas, Monet, Cassatt, and Remington. The Hancock Shaker Village near Pittsfield is an outstanding museum comprised of twenty buildings where you watch craftspeople weave baskets, make brooms, chairs, and oval Shaker boxes.

How to Get There.   From New York City take the Taconic State Parkway north to the Massachusetts Turnpike (I-90) east. From the Lee exit, take Route 20 to Route 7A north to Lenox. From Boston, take the Massachusetts Turnpike to the Lee exit.

Wheatleigh, *Lenox, Massachusetts*

Do thoughts of romance conjure up images of princesses and palaces? Have you often wondered how the Vanderbilt, Westinghouse, and Carnegie families spent their summers? Then plan a stay for a special occasion at this Florentine-inspired palace owned by Linfield and Susan Simon.

The circular driveway sets the stage with a porte-cochere entrance and fountain. In the great hall, carved reliefs of angels and cupids surround the baronial marble fireplace. A grand piano fits comfortably in one corner. The museum-quality collection of American ceramics is attractively offset by the eighteenth- and nineteenth-century English antiques in the front hall. The sweeping staircase and the captivating views of the Berkshire hills from the glass doors add to the magnificence of the setting. The atmosphere is formal. This is an elegant small hotel.

Here we found spacious accommodations, lots of privacy, as well as a dining experience second to none. The building now is air-conditioned throughout and there are phones in all the rooms. The master bedrooms have an airy, uncluttered feel that some guests love and others find too stark. The rooms with the best views are the five large ones on the second floor that overlook the hills and the one room on the first floor that looks out on the pool and the sculpture garden. Each of these rooms has a fireplace that uses Duraflame logs, and five also have balconies. The former quarters of the original owners, the Count and Countess de Heredia, have been converted into three of the grand second-floor rooms. One has a king-size bed with a canopy and another has two double beds; each has a large bath with an old-fashioned tub. The center room, the most interesting architecturally, has a dome ceiling and curved walls. The two corner second-floor rooms have covered balconies and king-size beds.

Another interesting accommodation with a more rustic feel, available only in the summer, is a duplex with a narrow spiral staircase. Leonard Bernstein used to stay here, and Rudolph Serkin even had his grand piano moved in. The living room is on the first floor and the bath and bedroom, which has two twin beds (the staircase is too narrow to bring up a larger bed), is on the second floor.

The mid-price-range rooms are quite spacious. As is the case in other mansions of the era, small rooms which might formerly have been used as servants' quarters have been converted into guest rooms. The prices, while far lower than the other rooms, are still relatively high since you are paying for the use of the common areas. The best of the lower-priced choices is a first-floor room with a high ceiling, a queen-size bed, and French doors opening onto the portico. To avoid disappointment ask about the size of the room before you make your reservation.

Landscaped by Frederick Law Olmsted, the genius behind
New York City's Central Park, the twenty-two wooded acres
are planted with thousands of spring bulbs. Paths through the
sculpture garden lead to an oval-shaped swimming pool set in a
grove of towering pines. The 100-year-old rock garden, newly
refurbished, is another quiet retreat. There is also a tennis court
on the property. And, of course, the fall foliage is spectacular in
the Berkshires. The inn's service area is visible as you approach
the front entrance, but cannot be seen from the gardens. The
back of the inn has magnificent views of the Berkshire hills.

Dinner here is likely to be one of the most romantic experiences you'll ever have. The dining room is elegantly appointed
with a pair of antique Waterford chandeliers and two matching
candelabra that flicker above the glowing fireplace. The tables
are set with a candle, fresh flowers, and white linen; the service
is impeccable.

We enjoyed a tasting dinner that was unforgettable and well
worth the price: it included two appetizers, sorbet, entrée,
salad, fruit and cheese, and a dessert sampler, followed by
coffee and a plate of such sweets as homemade truffles, cookies,
candied fruit, and a mini cream puff. Each dish was beautifully
coordinated with the china on which it was served. The caviar,
for example, was formed in the shape of a heart and served with
dollar-size blini on china decorated with a rose pattern.

The regular prix fixe dinner includes appetizers with choices
such as caviar with buckwheat blini as described above, a salad
of lobster and greens with mango ginger sauce, tempura of soft-
shelled crabs, sautéed sea scallops with papaya chutney and
coconut sauce, and a soup of red and yellow peppers with medallions of lobster.

Entrées feature Texas antelope with black huckleberries;
grilled striped bass with little-neck clams; poached halibut with
black trumpet mushrooms; and loin of veal with wild mushrooms
and sweetbread ravioli.

Desserts are exotic as well, and are beautifully presented: lemon mousse in a crisp pastry shell with fresh cherries; puff pastry and berries with vanilla ice cream; crèpes tagliatelle cut into wide strips with chocolate ice cream and orange sauce; sweetened framboise-scented chèvre and raspberries in a delicate pastry; or a selection of homemade sorbets. The dining room at Wheatleigh is one of the top restaurants in Massachusetts and should not be missed. The gala New Year's Eve dinner is the culinary highlight of the year.

A second dining option during the summer is The Grill Room. In nice weather, dining on the portico takes advantage of the mountain views. Everything is priced a la carte so you can have a snack or a full meal. Selections include Thai-style free range chicken, bouillabaisse, grilled salmon or swordfish, and a smoked turkey sandwich on sourdough bread.

Seventeen rooms in summer, sixteen rooms at other times of the year, each with private bath. July and August, Thursday through Sunday, $165-$425; three-night minimum stay on weekends. Midweek during the summer and the rest of the year, $110-$275; two-night minimum stay on weekends. There is an extensive a la carte breakfast menu. Dinner daily May through October, 6 to 9 P.M.; during Tanglewood season, 5 to 9 or 9:30 P.M. Lunch, brunch, and afternoon cocktails served during the summer in The Grill Room. November through April, dinner served Friday through Sunday; call about midweek days. Prix fixe, $65; tasting dinner, $90. Grill Room entrées, $9.50-$24. West Hawthorne Street (off Route 183), Lenox, MA 01240; (413) 637-0610.

What to Do. For more than fifty years, the Boston Symphony Orchestra at Tanglewood has been a major force in turning the Berkshire region into one of the great summer arts destinations in the country. More than 40 cultural organizations offer performances during the summer. Not only does the Boston

Symphony Orchestra perform during July and August at Tanglewood, but fine chamber music, choral music, theater, and dance are all available nearby. The Norman Rockwell Museum, with more than 600 of his paintings and drawings, is located in Stockbridge. Herman Melville wrote *Moby Dick* at Arrowhead, his home, which is located outside Pittsfield. The Clark Art Institute in Williamstown has an outstanding collection of seventeenth- through nineteenth-century paintings, including works by Gainsborough, Rembrandt, Renoir, Degas, Monet, Cassatt, and Remington. The Hancock Shaker Village near Pittsfield is an outstanding museum comprising twenty buildings where you can watch craftspeople weave baskets, make brooms, chairs, and oval Shaker boxes.

How to Get There. From Boston take the Massachusetts Turnpike west to the Lee exit. Go north on Route 20 to Route 7A into Lenox. In Lenox, go west on Route 183, then left onto West Hawthorne Street (just beyond Tanglewood). From New York City take the Taconic State Parkway north to the Massachusetts Turnpike, east to the Lee exit.

Yankee Clipper Inn, *Rockport, Massachusetts*

An inn that gives you a full ocean view from your room has a magnetic appeal. In our room at the Yankee Clipper we could watch the sun rise, see gulls glide by at eye level, observe lobstermen setting and checking their traps, and fall asleep to the sound of waves lapping against the shore. This prime oceanfront property, a mile north of the center of Rockport in a section called Pigeon Cove, has been owned and operated for more than forty years by the same family. Carrying on the tradition are innkeepers Barbara and Bob Ellis.

Our favorite rooms are located in the three-story building called the Quarterdeck. These rooms have picture windows and are slightly closer to the water than the main inn, so you really have the feeling of being at sea. Although the Oriental Room is not one of the large ones, it is the only room in which you can see the sun rise over the ocean from the bed. Golden State, a thirty-foot-long room with a wall of picture windows, has two double beds and is the only room on the top floor. Young America, a spacious room on the first floor, has a king-size bed, a living room with a pair of couches, and two picture windows with wonderful ocean views. Neptune's Car, a little smaller than Young America, has two picture windows, one looking toward the main inn and one looking toward the water; a king-size bed, and Queen Anne–style furnishings.

The main inn was built in 1929 as a private summer residence. The living room has fine carved molding, a pair of sofas, and a big fireplace. In the winter, guests gather here in the late afternoon to enjoy hot mulled cider and snacks.

We like the big rooms on the third floor in the summer months, as they have open porches and excellent views of the rocky shore. Two rooms with spectacular open private decks are Volunteer, with a king-size bed and lovely Chinese lamps that match the wallpaper, and Sovereign of the Sea, one of the largest rooms, with two antique double sleigh beds.

The best rooms on the second floor have glass-enclosed porches with windows that can be opened. Flying Cloud, the master bedroom in days gone by, has a king-size bed, a chaise longue, and new wicker furniture on the porch. Red Jacket has a double and a twin bed; the newly winterized porch has floor-to-ceiling windows and antique blue wicker furniture. Sea Witch has a queen-size bed with a fishnet canopy. This room has the largest enclosed porch in the inn and is furnished with a convertible couch and off-white wicker furniture with cushions.

Across the street is the more traditional Bullfinch House, built as a private home in 1840. The rooms here are nicely decorated with antiques but do not have water views. These are the lowest-priced rooms.

The inn has a heated salt-water swimming pool and a rocky bluff, a perfect spot for ocean-gazing and watching the lobstermen.

A full breakfast includes a choice of a hot entrée such as blueberry pancakes; poached eggs with spinach basil sauce served in puff pastry; Belgian waffles with strawberries or other seasonal fruit and whipped cream. Also included is an extensive buffet table of fruit juices, fresh fruit, muffins, sweet breads, and cold cereals.

The Glass Verandah, the restaurant at the Yankee Clipper Inn, features New England cuisine with an emphasis on local seafood. Dining is at tables along a glass wall with spectacular views of the water. The specialty is stuffed lobster Verandah, lobster tail meat mixed with scallops, mushrooms, and a light cream sauce, then baked in the shell with Parmesan cheese. Other specialities include shrimp sautéed with apple chutney and mustard, seafood au gratin, and poached salmon filet with red pepper sauce. Also on the menu is a vegetarian stir-fry, veal marsala, and stir-fried beef tenderloin.

Twenty-seven rooms and suites, all with private bath. Memorial Day through mid-October, $99–$196. Other times of the year: weekends, $99–$130, midweek, $69–$99. Full breakfast included on weekends and during the summer. Continental buffet breakfast served midweek during the off-season. 15% service charge on breakfast only. Children over age 3 welcome. Third person in room, $25. No pets. Dinner served daily Memorial Day through the third weekend of October; Friday and Saturday during the rest of the year, 5:30 to 9 P.M. Entrées, $13.95–$21.95. Box 2399, 96 Granite Street, Rockport, MA 01966; (800) 545-3699 or (508) 546-3407.

Where to Dine.   The Glass Verandah restaurant at Yankee Clipper Inn features New England cuisine, and the porch window tables have wonderful views of the rocky coastline.

Bistro, at 2 Main Street in Gloucester (508-281-8055), serves highly creative dishes that draw from the cuisines of Asia, the Southwest, and Italy. We enjoyed the paper-thin slices of gingered beef carpaccio and chili rellenos stuffed with black beans and cheese. Marinated fork-tender seared pork was served with Hunan barbecue sauce and spicy twice-fried potatoes.

When you're looking for romantic surroundings and fine

French-style cooking, go to The White Rainbow in Gloucester (65 Main Street, downstairs; 508-281-0017) and try the lobster stew for two, a rich combination of heavy cream, brandy, spices and fresh lobster meat. For lunch, visit the Halibut Point Restaurant in Gloucester (289 Main Street; 508-281-1900) for a spicy tomato-based Italian fish soup filled with chunks of tomatoes, vegetables, and fish.

What to Do.   Artists by the hundreds flock to Cape Ann to capture their impressions of this glorious seascape. You'll see many fine examples of their work at the galleries at the Rocky Neck Art Colony in East Gloucester. The Rockport Art Association has 250 artist members who show their work at different shows throughout the year. The Cape Ann Historical Association has a large collection of paintings by Fitz Hugh Lane, the master nautical and luminist painter of the mid-nineteenth century.

Go whale watching from Gloucester. Tour the medieval-style Hammond Castle that sits on the water's edge and catch an organ recital in the 100-foot-long Great Hall. Browse the shops along Bearskin Neck in Rockport, or relax on one of the white sand beaches in Rockport or Gloucester.

How to Get There.   From Boston, take Route 128 north to Cape Ann. Continue on Route 128 through the first rotary (first exit for Route 127) and the second rotary. Turn left at the next exit (Route 127, Eastern Avenue) and drive four miles to Rockport. Continue on Route 127 through Rockport. The road makes a sharp left turn and is now called Granite Street. The inn is about one and a half miles farther along the road.

Watermark Inn, *Provincetown, Massachusetts*

Watermark Inn is the perfect place in Provincetown if you want to stay directly on the water, watch the sun rise, or listen to the rhythmic pounding of the sea. At high tide the water comes to the edge of the decks outside the rooms, and at low tide the inn has a private sand beach. To your right, you can see the fishing boats and whale-watching boats coming into and departing from Provincetown's harbor. To the left, you can see the lights of Truro and Wellfleet. The Watermark is located in an area known as the "quiet East End," a fifteen-minute walk from the center of the town's commercial district.

The inn is owned by Kevin Shea and Judy Richland. DeeAnn Paris, the resident innkeeper, is the person who will greet you and give pointers about restaurants and things to do. This is the kind of inn where guests are left to their own schedule. Arising early and taking a walk down Commercial Street with a stop for breakfast at one of the coffee shops or Portuguese bakeries, we enjoyed the freedom from planned meals and dining hours. A wide variety of restaurants, markets, and bakeries are within walking distance from the inn.

The sleek, spacious, contemporary suites feature skylights and angled ceilings. The second-floor suites have triangular windows and furnishings follow crisp, uncluttered Scandinavian-style lines. Colorful contemporary designer quilts contrast with the white walls and furniture, which is upholstered in shades of gray and white. Six of the ten suites have sliding glass doors opening onto a shared deck. Two have working fireplaces that use Duraflame logs. Some offer full front views of the water, while others have partial water views. All have cable television, telephones, and tiled baths. One suite has a full kitchen; the others have kitchenettes with a sink, small refrigerator, coffee maker, and toaster oven.

An oceanfront location provides dramatic views during a storm. Although a storm in late 1990 swept through Provincetown at the worst possible time (high tide and a full moon) and caused damage to the four first-floor waterfront suites, Kevin, an architect, took it all in stride. To him the damage was an opportunity to do some renovations, which included refinishing floors and adding new rugs and window coverings.

We favor suites with decks that look out over the water. Our favorite first-floor suite, #3, is the largest suite and is popular with guests who do not want to climb stairs. Its living room has twelve feet of glass, opening onto the deck with a full front water view. Furnishings include a king-size bed and a working fireplace.

The second-floor suites have particularly spectacular water views because of their wider panorama, but the rooms are slightly smaller than those on the first floor. The second-floor deck is set back farther from the water to prevent shading the deck below it. Suite 7, a corner suite, looks west out over the Provincetown harbor. It has a full kitchen and a king-size bed. Suite 8 is a favorite with honeymooners for its working fireplace, located directly across the room from the queen-size bed. Suite 10, a corner suite with a queen-size bed, faces east—perfect for watching the sunrise. If lying in bed and listening to the waves appeals to you, this is the suite where ocean sounds are loudest.

Other suites with full front water views and decks are #4 (first floor) and #9 (second floor). Lower-priced suites 1 and 2 look out onto an interior courtyard; #5 and #6 have partial water views.

Ten suites, each with private bath. Six with water views, two with fireplaces. July through Labor Day, $110–$245. Other times of the year, $60–$185. Higher rates on holiday weekends. Children welcome. Additional charge for third or fourth person in the room. Three- or four-night minimum stay on holiday weekends. Meals not included. No pets. 603 Commercial Street, Provincetown, MA 02657; (800) 734-0165 (Massachusetts only) or (508) 487-0165.

Where to Dine. For fine dining in Provincetown we suggest the Front Street Restaurant, especially for the delicate leek-and-lobster bisque or the baked artichoke stuffed with bread crumbs and sausage (230 Commercial Street; 508-487-9715). Try Napi's (7 Freeman Street; 508-487-1145) for Wellfleet oysters or the Portuguese platter made with half a lobster, littleneck clams, mussels, fresh fish, and *linguica* sausage smothered in a thick spicy sauce. The Moors (Bradford Street West; 508-487-0840) has hearty Portuguese soup made with cabbage and spicy *chourico* sausage.

Ciro and Sal's, with exceptional northern Italian cooking, has a large wood-burning fireplace and low ceilings (430 Commercial Street; 508-487-0049). The tender calamari were sautéed with whole anchovies, lemon, garlic, and cream.

Café Edwige (333 Commercial Street; 508-487-2008) is a good choice for breakfast. The legendary Danish pastry is flaky, buttery, and has a mouthwatering filling (the day we dined it was raspberry cream cheese). Pucci's Harborside (539 Commercial Street; 508-487-1964) is a casual restaurant where you can practically feel the water as it laps against the pilings at high tide. It features reasonably priced American food.

What to Do.   Provincetown is three miles long and two to three streets wide. This liberal, closely knit community boasts a fascinating cosmopolitan mix of arts-oriented people. The whale-watching fleet, the largest on the East Coast, attracts many visitors to town, as do to a lesser extent the artists and writers who have made this the most famous art colony in the country. There are fine galleries and shops along Commercial Street. The scenery at this tip of Cape Cod is different from anything else you will see in the United States. Fishermen of Portuguese descent leave early each morning in their colorful boats from the end of MacMillan Wharf and return in the afternoon to unload their catch of cod, mackerel, and flounder. Come during any season of the year and nature displays its power along the forty-mile-long Cape Cod National Seashore. Giant sand dunes encroach on the highway near Provincetown. The Province Lands Trail is an eight-mile paved bicycle path that goes through the dunes in the Provincetown section of the Cape Cod National Seashore. Race Point and Herring Cove beaches are nearby. You get a spectacular view of the tip of Cape Cod from the top of the 252-foot-tall Pilgrim Monument, a replica of a Siena bell tower, and you can see recently discovered pirate treasure in the museum.

How to Get There.   From the Bourne or Sagamore bridges at the beginning of the Cape, take Route 6 directly to Provincetown and turn left at the the first exit, which is marked "East End." Turn right onto Route 6A. Bear left at the fork onto Commercial Street. Stay on the waterside road. The inn is on the left less than a mile down the road.

The Wauwinet, *Nantucket, Massachusetts*

In the quiet isolation of a setting bounded by the Atlantic Ocean on one side and Nantucket harbor on the other, just nine miles from the center of town, the Wauwinet is a truly deluxe, full-service inn. No expense has been spared to create a magnificent showplace. The decor includes exquisite bouquets of fresh flowers, gorgeous chintz fabrics, whimsical trompe l'oeil floors, antique scrimshaw, original Audubon elephant folio prints, fine oil paintings, bronze sculptures—the list could go on and on. While this is an extraordinarily expensive inn, we were impressed to find none of the stuffy formality that is common at other grand hotels.

The most romantic accommodations are the spacious bay-view rooms with full panoramic views of the inn's private beach, Nantucket harbor, and a partial view of the ocean. Have room service deliver a bottle of champagne and sip it in the privacy of your grand room as you watch the changing shades of the sunset. (This narrow strip of Nantucket, which faces west, is one of the few spots on the East Coast where you can watch the sun set over the water.)

Each of the thirty-two rooms is individually decorated in a French country style, with old pine armoires and chests, easy chairs, light-brown sisal rugs, baskets, and old hatboxes. The beds are covered with designer comforters; sheets and pillow cases are eyelet trimmed; and the dust ruffles match the upholstery.

While all the rooms are decorated with the same attention to detail, prices vary widely. The cottage rooms do not have harbor views; midsize rooms, called superior rooms, have partial water views; and the deluxe rooms, the largest, have panoramic views of the water. There are twenty-nine rooms in the main inn and eleven rooms spread among five cottages. A cottage suite accommodates from four to eight persons and includes a fireplace and a kitchen.

Some of the more unusual breakfast choices included granola with whole hazelnuts, and the wild mushroom omelet made with just the egg whites.

Guests at the Wauwinet are taken for a complimentary boat cruise around the harbor. Also included in the room rate is use of the inn's two tennis courts, Sunfish, rowing shells, fishing rods, and bicycles. An almost hourly jitney service takes guests from the inn into town. The concierge can also make arrangements for Jeep rentals or guided tours of the island.

Toppers is in our opinion one of the top two restaurants on an island, known for its gourmet fare featuring new American cuisine. Three intimate dining rooms are decorated with oversized baskets of fresh flowers. Couches, pillow-covered wicker chairs, and upholstered armchairs surround white linen-covered tables, comfortably spaced for ease of conversation and a relaxing ambience.

The most popular appetizer is crabcakes made from Chesapeake Bay jumbo lump crabmeat. The Nantucket seafood chowder here is a delicate blending of smoked seafood in a rich cream broth. Entrée portions are exceptionally large and served with imaginative side dishes that are practically a meal in themselves. The tuna was served with a lobster-avocado burrito, paper-thin homemade potato chips, and locally grown baby carrots and squash. The roasted monkfish and large pieces of lobster tail came with shredded potato pancakes, baby beets, and zucchini and carrots, as well as crispy fried leek slivers. The grilled rack and leg of lamb were served with wedges of gratinéed potatoes, a tomato-eggplant timbale, and tender baby vegetables.

A scoop each of homemade blackberry and passion-mango sorbet came with a selection of crisp butter cookies. The traditional blueberry pie with vanilla ice cream was outstanding, as was the dense chocolate cognac cake. Coffee is served with chocolate candies.

Open mid-May through October. Thirty-two rooms, each with private bath. From mid-June through mid-September: rooms, $250–$620, cottage suites, $540–$995. Other times of the year: rooms, $220–$450, cottage suites, $360–$895. Continental breakfast included. There is a minimum three-night stay for weekends in July and August and holiday weekends. Inquire about package plans. Toppers is open daily for breakfast, lunch, afternoon snacks, and dinner. Advance dinner reservations required. Lunch entrées, $9–$15; dinner entrées, $22–$32. Box 2580, Nantucket, MA 02584; (800) 426-8718 or (508) 228-0145.

What to Do. The Wauwinet will arrange for a skipper to take you to an isolated spot on Coatue, a remote part of the island, where you can enjoy the privacy of the beach and a custom-created gourmet picnic. You can bicycle to Siasconset or to Madaket, shop for lightship baskets, and visit the whaling museum or other historic sites. Rent a Jeep to drive on the sand to Great Point, one of the best spots on the island for fishing and also one of the prettiest. Sailing and tennis are available at the inn, or just spend your days at the beach.

How to Get There. Take the ferry from Hyannis, a two-and-a-half-hour trip, or fly from Hyannis, New Bedford, Boston, or New York.

JANE STAUFFER

Cliffside Inn, *Newport, Rhode Island*

The Cliffside Inn is located on a quiet residential street about a fifteen-minute walk from the harbor area, and less than a two-minute walk from the famed Cliff Walk. We found the large living room, painted and trimmed in shades of rose and green, to be a very welcoming spot, decorated with color-coordinated Victorian couches and easy chairs, a wood-burning fireplace, tables for games and puzzles, a bay-window seat, a stereoscopic viewer, even an old Australian phone booth. In the late afternoon, hot or cold beverages and hors d'oeuvres such as curry or a hot artichoke dip are served around the fireplace or, in summer, on the wide wicker-filled front porch.

The most romantic room is Miss Beatrice's, where you can get the best winter view looking toward the ocean. The bedroom has a Victorian window seat, a queen-size bed with a walnut headboard, a wood burning fireplace, and the largest bath in the house, which includes a whirlpool tub and an oversized shower with two shower heads large enough for two people to shower together.

The Turner Suite on the third floor has a queen-size rosewood bed with a half-canopy and a separate sitting room with a love-seat. The bath has a double whirlpool tub with a hand-held shower. There are skylights in the bedroom, sitting room, and bath.

The Attic Room, constructed on the third floor by raising the roof and adding three skylights, is a bedroom with a cathedral ceiling and king-size bed, an antique mirror-front armoire, and two easy chairs. French doors open onto the bathroom, which is lined with mirrors and has a whirlpool tub, a separate shower, and a skylight.

The Governor's Suite includes a large living room with a chintz-covered couch, two wing-back chairs, a television, and a VCR. The small bedroom has a queen-size bed with an emerald green comforter and green and white trompe l'oeil wallpaper; the bath has a small deep whirlpool tub.

Miss Adele's Room has a carved oak high headboard on the queen-size bed, a matching oak dresser, a black marble wood burning fireplace, rocking chair, and a large bath.

The entrance to the smaller Veranda Room, which has a queen-size bed and a bath with a shower only, is off the front porch. Guests who are smokers and those who like greater privacy prefer this room because it has direct access to the porch, the only area where smoking is permitted.

A full breakfast served from 8 to 10 A.M. by the resident innkeepers, Annette and Norbert Mede, includes freshly squeezed orange juice, fresh fruit, homemade granola, yogurt, muffins, and an entrée such as walnut pancakes, eggs Benedict, almond French toast, or bacon and leek quiche.

Twelve rooms with private bath, four with fireplaces, May through October, $125–$235. At other times of the year rates are lower midweek. Full breakfast included. Children over 13 welcome; $30 additional for a third person in the room. No pets. No smoking. Two Seaview Avenue, Newport, RI 02840; (800) 845-1811 or (401) 847-1811.

Where to Dine. For casual dining we can't get enough of the *lasagna di verdure* or the sweet red roasted peppers in oil and garlic at Puerini's (24 Memorial Boulevard; 401-847-5506). At Scales and Shells (527 Thames Street; 401-846-FISH), don't miss the lobster fra diavolo. The thick, spicy tomato sauce peppered with clams, mussels, squid, and lobster is served on a bed of linguine in a steaming hot frying pan.

For lunch or an afternoon snack get a bowl of thick pasta fagioli with Parmesan cheese and a cappuccino at Ocean Coffee Roaster (22 Washington Square; 401-846-6060). Formal dining is best at White Horse Tavern, America's oldest tavern, built in 1687 (Marlborough and Farewell Streets; 401-849-3600). Try the grilled lamb or veal chops.

What to Do. Newport is an area that you can return to time and again. If you choose, you can spend your entire stay indoors touring the mansions. The Breakers is the most opulent. Others along Bellevue Avenue include Marble House, Château-sur-Mer, The Elms, Rosecliff, Kingscote, and Belcourt Castle. The three-and-a-half-mile Cliff Walk is one of the most famous in America. On one side is a row of mansions like none other in existence, and on the other the mighty Atlantic pounds the rocky shoreline at your feet. The experience, especially the day after a storm, is unforgettable. You can head to the beach, drive or bike along ten-mile Ocean Drive and see more mansions, grand estates, and dramatic ocean views. Stop at Hammersmith Farm to see Jacqueline Kennedy Onassis's childhood bedroom and the office that President Kennedy used as his summer home away from Washington. Go antiquing, gallery hopping, and shopping.

Visit Green Animals, a topiary garden, or take a tour of Sakonnet vineyards. Take a harbor cruise, rent a sailboat, or simply find a spot near the water, watch the waves, and enjoy a good book.

How to Get There. From Boston, take I-93 south, then Route 24 south, to Route 114 south to Newport. Turn left on Memorial Drive, right on Cliff Avenue, left on Seaview Avenue. From New York City, take I-95 north to Rhode Island. Exit at Route 138 east into Newport. Turn left off Memorial Drive onto Cliff Avenue, left on Seaview Avenue.

The fireplace in the "keeping" room

Riverwind Inn, *Deep River, Connecticut*

What could be more fun than renewing your wedding vows at a romantic, much-photographed New England inn? Following the ceremony, a vintage Rolls-Royce whisks you off to a gourmet French dinner. Return to your room to sip champagne on your private porch, relax in the large soaking tub, or curl up in front of a blazing fireplace. This romantic inn is owned by Barbara Barlow, who also happens to be the local justice of the peace, and her husband, Bob Bucknall, who can always be counted on to be the witness.

Riverwind, less than a three-hour drive from New York City, is a jewel of Americana located in Deep River, a small town that hugs the banks of the lower Connecticut River. Here, eight rooms, along with eight common living rooms (four with wood-burning fireplaces), provide a luxurious amount of space for guests' use. The front parlor has a piano and a fireplace. The trophy room is guarded by George, the inn's resident stuffed deer, who watches over the antique checkerboard. The library is filled with books and magazines. A breathtaking twelve-foot stone cooking fireplace dominates the "keeping" room. Scattered throughout—hanging from rafters, tucked in corners, mounted on walls, and arranged on tables—is a striking collection of authentic American folk art. Of particular note are the dozen or so quilts collected from the hills of Virginia.

Each room has its own distinctive personality. Champagne and Roses, the honeymoon suite, is named for the complimentary bottle of champagne and the rose patterns on the sheets, the carpets, and decorating the bath. The colors of the rose garden, viewed from your private porch, skillfully coordinate with the colors of the room.

Our second romantic choice is Zelda's, a cozy emerald-green suite furnished in glowing oak. The old brass daybed in the sitting room is covered with a delicate heirloom lace spread and topped with an abundance of equally lacy pillows. A massive carved oak bed dominates the small bedroom and an old stained-glass window glows in the bath. The Willow Room has a seventeenth-century bird's eye maple four-poster double bed and a private porch.

Hearts and Flowers is decorated in French country style, with a white iron and brass queen-size bed and an antique pine armoire. The Barn Rose Room, one of the lower-priced rooms, has a fishnet canopy over a four-poster bed.

During our stay Barbara's cheery hospitality made us feel happy and carefree. She does everything she can to brighten your stay, right down to jumping at any excuse to light one of the four fireplaces. This is an inn where, with a mug of mulled cider from the black pot heating over the fire, we happily sit back and let the worries of the world slip away.

At breakfast, she fires up the stove and prepares a real country breakfast in a real country kitchen. And what a kitchen it is—dripping with hanging pots, hams, old biscuit barrels, lard cans, tobacco tins, molds, and cooking contraptions of every shape and size. Amid the smells of baking biscuits and wood burning in the fireplace, we sat down to a spread of Smithfield ham, homemade piglet-shaped biscuits, pastries, fruit, and a hot vegetarian casserole that combined artichoke hearts, asparagus, tomatoes, mushrooms, and eggs.

Six rooms, each with private bath, $90–$110; two suites, $130–$155. Full breakfast included. Children over 12 welcome. No pets. 209 Main Street, Deep River, CT 06417; (203) 526-2014.

Where to Dine.   The Post and Beam restaurant at the Inn at Chester (318 West Main Street, Route 156; 203-526-1307) with creative American cuisine is a top choice. Try the Mediterranean salad appetizer, mussel stew, the shrimp and linguine, or swordfish served with orange-basil oil.

Restaurant du Village in Chester (59 Main Street; 203-526-5301) serves excellent country French cuisine. Try the cassoulet or the meat stew. The fruit soufflé and the genoise are good choices for dessert.

8 Westbrook (203-767-7085) has only twenty-four seats in a converted Colonial farmhouse in Centerbrook and serves specialities such as Thai marinated shrimp, calf's liver with orange

and hazelnut sauce, and fettuccine topped with crayfish and wild mushrooms.

Fine Bouche (18 Main Street, Centerbrook; 203-767-1277) is particularly known for its excellent wine list, its strawberry-honeydew soup, and rack of lamb with fresh tarragon and mustard sauce. Copper Beach Inn (Main Street, Ivoryton; 203-767-0330) has a rich lobster bisque and an excellent rack of lamb. The desserts are legendary here: try the white chocolate mousse in a pastry tulip. For seafood, go to Fiddlers (4 Water Street, Chester; 203-526-3210). For a full meal or an appetizer, try the Chart House, which has a lounge overlooking a waterfall (129 West Main Street, Route 156, Chester; 203-526-9898), or the Griswold Inn, a veritable institution in Essex that is well past its 200th anniversary (48 Main Street; 203-767-1812).

What to Do. You must reserve ahead for the popular musical productions at the picturesque six-story Victorian Goodspeed Opera House in East Haddam, where *Man of La Mancha, Shenandoah*, and *Annie* got their starts. Take the little Chester-Hadlyme ferry across the Connecticut River. Visit the Rhennish-style Gillette Castle, perched 200 feet above the Connecticut River. From the castle, take Joshuatown Road to Route 156 south to Old Lyme for a visit to the Florence Griswold Museum, known for its outstanding collection of American Impressionist paintings. Take a cruise on the Connecticut River; boats leave from Haddam.

How to Get There. From New York City take I-95, the Connecticut Turnpike, north to the Route 9 exit at Old Saybrook. Take Route 9 north to exit 4, then Route 154 north to Deep River. From Boston take I-95 south to Route 9 north, then follow the above directions.

JANE STAUFFER

Manor House, *Norfolk, Connecticut*

As a house present in 1898, Louis Tiffany installed twenty stained-glass windows in this handsome Victorian Tudor-style home set on five acres in the quiet town of Norfolk, in northwestern Connecticut. Thanks to his generosity, today you can sit at the breakfast table or by the fireplace and admire the shades of blue, yellow, and green shell and fleur-de-lis–patterned windows.

Innkeepers Diane and Hank Tremblay have created a casual yet elegant atmosphere in their sizeable home. The grand living room is dominated by a mammoth raised fireplace decorated with a bas-relief of a figure driving his chariot and horses, surrounded by sofas and easy chairs that invite you to spend hours reading or listening to selections from the Tremblays' extensive collection of compact discs. A grand piano sits ready for an impromptu concert. There is a library room filled to overflowing with books, a porch room, and picnic-perfect grounds enclosed by a 600-foot stone wall, with professionally designed perennial borders, beehives, and a raspberry patch.

The thirty-by-eighteen-foot Spofford Room (the largest) has windows on three sides draped with lacy curtains. A king-size bed with an old lace canopy fills one end of the room; a wood-burning fireplace and chairs fill the other. An outside deck overlooking the grounds is an ideal spot for a private breakfast.

The newly redone, oversized English Room is a combination bedroom and bath with a king-size bed, a Jacuzzi, and a separate shower.

The Country French Room on the third floor has an old brass queen-size bed. The large bath with cedar walls and ceiling includes a soaking tub big enough for two.

The Lincoln Room, although one of the smallest, has a fireplace and a good view of the grounds (which are pastel soft with apple blossoms in spring). It has a double antique sleigh bed with elaborate carvings and a white fainting couch.

The Balcony Room is among the smaller rooms but it is a good choice for the summer, as it has a private deck. A wood-paneled elevator, added to the house in 1931 and still in good running order, is used to reach this room.

Guests can have breakfast served to them in their room or join other guests in the dining room. Breakfast includes a choice of two entrées such as orange waffles, poached eggs with lemon butter and chive sauce on English muffins, or blueberry pancakes. During breakfast we enjoyed both the honey and Hank's detailed explanation of beekeeping.

Eight rooms, all with private bath, $90–$150. Full breakfast included. Children over eight welcome. Third person in room, $20 additional. No pets. Two-night minimum stay on weekends during the summer and fall. No smoking. Maple Avenue, Box 447, Norfolk, CT 06058; (203) 542-5690.

Where to Dine. For elegant dining in an historic Colonial atmosphere, go to the Inn on the Green in nearby New Marlborough, Massachusetts (413-229-3131) for a candlelight dinner. The Creole spice shrimp, grilled baby chicken, and loin of veal with braised mustard greens and wild mushrooms are favorites. The Cannery in Canaan (85 Main Street, Route 44; 203-824-7333) is a casual small café specializing in Cajun cooking such as crawfish and oyster étouffée, blackened catfish, or jambalaya for two served in a large sizzling cast-iron pan filled with shrimp, spicy tasso ham, andouille (Cajun smoked pork) sausage, and chicken.

Julie's New American Sea Grill at The White Hart Inn in Salisbury (203-435-0030) specializes in seafood such as pan-seared, peppercorn-encrusted loin of tuna or sautéed sea scallops served on fresh garlic tagliatelle.

Freshfields in West Cornwall (Route 128; 203-672-6601) has spectacular porch tables that overlook a rushing stream. Under Mountain Inn (482 Under Mountain Road, Route 41, Salisbury; 203-435-0242) serves excellent British food such as steak and kidney pie or fish and chips as good as or better than what you can get in London.

The Gilson Café and Cinema in Winsted (Route 44; 203-379-5108) is a restored Art Deco theater with little café tables that allow you to watch a movie while enjoying a light supper of seafood-stuffed pita bread, a bowl of chili, or beef stew.

What to Do. The inn is just a short walk from the seventy-acre estate where the Yale Music School has its summer music institute and presents the Norfolk Chamber Music Festival in July. Forty-five minutes to the north is Tanglewood, where the Boston Symphony Orchestra performs for thousands during July and August. Hillside Gardens in Norfolk is one of the finest perennial gardens in the United States. The area is full of antique shops and old bookstores. North of Norfolk is the old Buggy Whip factory, now home to thirty-eight antique dealers.

West Cornwall has a beautiful one-lane covered bridge over the Housatonic River. Barbara Farnsworth's store of the same name has some 50,000 old books. Ian Ingersoll is one of the best handcrafted-furniture makers in New England, with Shaker reproductions his specialty.

Drive over to Salisbury, another lovely small New England town, and stop for excellent tea and cake at Chaiwalla Tea Room.

Continue south to Litchfield, one of the finest examples of a late eighteenth-century town with its green, its tall, spired church, and grand eighteenth- and nineteenth-century homes. Drive west to New Preston and have a look at a dozen or so upscale antique stores and drive around beautiful Lake Waramaug.

How to Get There. From New York take I-84 east to Waterbury, Connecticut, and head north on Route 8. At Winsted take Route 44 west to Norfolk. From Massachusetts take the Massachusetts Turnpike exit for Route 7 south to Canaan. Then go east on Route 44 to Norfolk.

JANE STAUFFER

The Mayflower Inn, *Washington, Connecticut*

Twenty-eight acres of formal gardens, mountain streams, specimen trees, and hundred-year-old rhododendrons form the backdrop to this exquisite country-house hotel. As you walk the grounds and through the common rooms you will sense the high standards and good taste of the owners, Adriana and Robert Mnuchin. Since the original 1920 Mayflower Inn was in poor repair, the Mnuchins rebuilt it on the same site and added two additional guest houses, a conference center, tennis court, swimming pool, and fitness center.

The new inn opened in March 1992, but the combination of antiques throughout the common rooms, along with Oriental rugs, walnut and mahogany paneling, fine oil paintings, and decorative pieces, lend the patina of age. We particularly liked the richly paneled library with a fireplace, furnished with a leather sofa and chairs, a window seat, and shelves of artfully arranged books including many first editions.

Each designer-decorated room is spacious and includes a pair of upholstered easy chairs or a sofa. Most rooms have a king-size carved four-poster bed with a featherbed on top of the mattress and soft 320-thread-count Italian Frette sheets. The oversize baths have mahogany paneling, double marble-topped sinks, a glass-enclosed tiled shower, and a deep soaking tub. The price variation between the rooms is naturally reflected by the size, whether there's a balcony, and whether the rooms look onto the flower gardens or the woods. There are fifteen rooms and suites in the main inn and five in each of the other two buildings. There is also a heated swimming pool, a tennis court, and a health center with a full selection of machines, aerobic classes, and two masseurs on staff.

Before dinner, take a stroll of the manicured grounds and the exquisitely furnished common rooms. Then have a drink on the grand white wicker–filled porch that wraps around two sides of the main building.

In warm weather you can dine on the outdoor terrace overlooking the Shakespearean garden. The three elegant dining rooms have widely spaced tables where your conversation is not likely to be easily overheard. Tables are set with Irish linen and French Limoges china that was designed for the inn. Nineteenth-century oil paintings decorate the walls of the dining room and are found throughout the inn.

Service is friendly, attentive but not fussy. For starters we recommend the cream of lobster soup with pieces of lobster mushroom (a bright orange-red wild mushroom) laced with Armagnac, which had an intense flavor. A small gourmet pizza is usually on the menu, such as one with pieces of poultry sausage, fontina and taleggio cheeses. The chef has a fondness for orecchiette (cup-shape) pasta which we had with wild mushrooms and arugula as an entrée. Earlier in the season the pasta was served with duck bolognese sauce and spinach. The large portion of mixed greens was tossed with a very light chardonnay vinaigrette.

A large grilled veal chop cooked medium rare to our request had a robust flavor and was served with whole wheat pasta and a chunky mushroom sauce. The well-prepared breast of chicken was served with the chicken leg cooked confit style and a generous portion of real (not instant) mashed potatoes. The more flavorful ballotine of boned rabbit (a scalloppine rolled around a loin, tied, then roasted and served on top of a savory summer vegetable stew) was a good choice. Atlantic halibut was grilled and accompanied with a tomato cucumber relish and new potatoes roasted with saffron. An extensive, reasonably priced wine list is backed with a cellar of more than 7,000 bottles as well as forty wines available by the glass.

Top choices on the dessert menu include a large cookie shell filled with intensely flavored scoops of watermelon, raspberry, and blackberry ices, and a crunchy caramel peach sundae topped with honey crème fraîche.

Seventeen rooms, $190–$275, and seven suites, $285–$475, all with private bath. Meals available but are not included. Children over 12 welcome. No pets. Two-night minimum on weekends; three nights on holiday weekends. Lunch daily, 12 to 2:30 P.M., $7.25–$11.50. Dinner nightly, 6 to 9:30 P.M. Entrées,

$14.50–$24. Bar Room open until midnight. Route 47, Washington, CT 06793; (203) 868-9466.

What to Do. Drive to Litchfield, one of the finest examples of a late-eighteenth-century New England town with its town green, its tall, spired white church, and grand eighteenth- and nineteenth-century homes. Tour the gardens and the garden shop at White Flower Farm. Drive to New Preston and have a look at a dozen or so upscale antique stores and drive around beautiful Lake Waramaug. Canoe or fly-fish the Housatonic River. In Washington Depot, the Mendelson Gallery has shows of the finest collections of bowls, pots, and baskets by contemporary artisans. Have lunch at The Pantry, which is a combination cooking store and gourmet café. Visit the galleries in Kent, or the Eric Sloane museum featuring the artist's paintings and his early-American tool collection. In Kent Falls State Park, a path follows the 200-foot waterfall. West Cornwall has a beautiful one-lane covered bridge over the Housatonic River. Hillside Gardens in Norfolk is one of the finest perennial gardens in the United States. Drive over to Salisbury, another lovely small New England town, for excellent tea and cake at Chaiwalla Tea Room.

How to Get There. From I-84 at Danbury, take Route 202 north beyond New Milford. Take Route 109 east to Washington Depot. Go south on Route 47 to the inn.

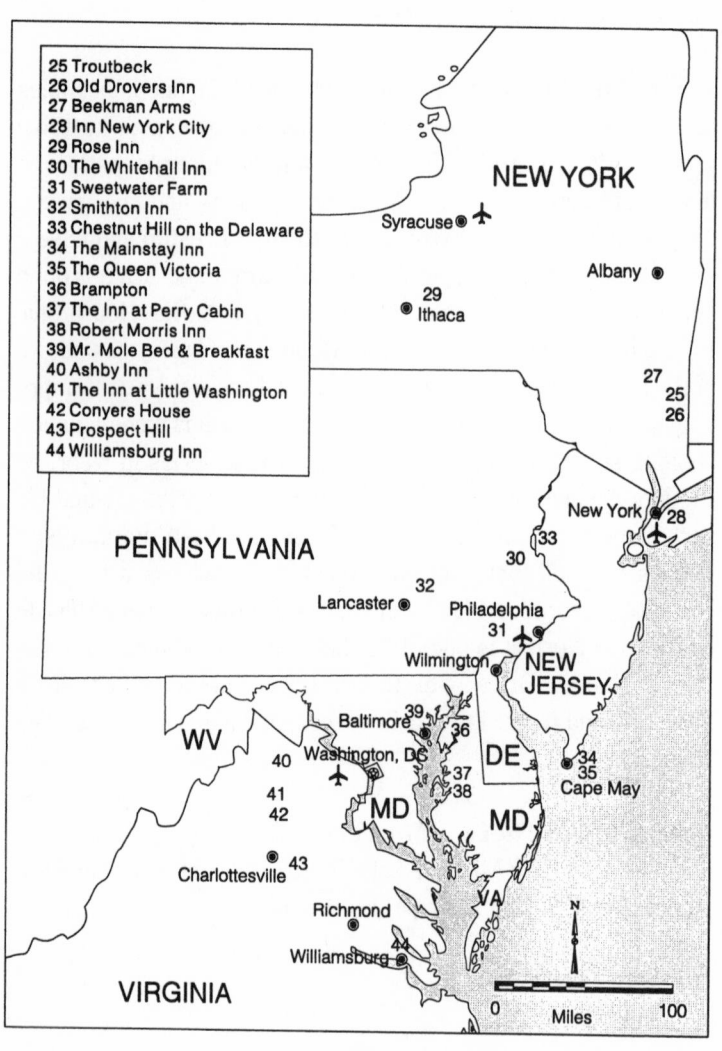

25 Troutbeck
26 Old Drovers Inn
27 Beekman Arms
28 Inn New York City
29 Rose Inn
30 The Whitehall Inn
31 Sweetwater Farm
32 Smithton Inn
33 Chestnut Hill on the Delaware
34 The Mainstay Inn
35 The Queen Victoria
36 Brampton
37 The Inn at Perry Cabin
38 Robert Morris Inn
39 Mr. Mole Bed & Breakfast
40 Ashby Inn
41 The Inn at Little Washington
42 Conyers House
43 Prospect Hill
44 Williamsburg Inn

NEW YORK

Syracuse

Albany

29
Ithaca

27
25
26

New York 28

PENNSYLVANIA

33

30

Lancaster 32

Philadelphia
31

NEW
JERSEY

Wilmington

Baltimore 39
36

WV

40 Washington, DC

DE 34
35
Cape May

41
42

MD

37
38

MD

Charlottesville 43

VA

Richmond

N

Williamsburg 44

VIRGINIA

0   Miles   100

Troutbeck, *Amenia, New York*

From Monday through Friday, this 440-acre English-style country estate is a conference center catering to only one corporate group at a time. On most weekends of the year (when not booked for a wedding), the property operates as a country inn from 5 P.M. Friday through 2 P.M. Sunday. The estate is a secluded destination where you could spend the entire weekend without feeling the need to leave the property.

And what a property it is. Its history dates back to 1765, from 1910 to 1979 it was owned by Joel Spingarn, a famous critic, poet, and philosopher, and his wife, Amy. During the 1920s, liberals and literati, including Sinclair Lewis, Louis Mumford, and the great Mexican muralist Orozco, spent weekends here. Troutbeck was also the site of conception for the NAACP. Since 1979 Jim Flaherty and Bob Skibsted have owned and operated this fabulous property.

A narrow, winding private road crosses a bubbling trout stream and winds its way through the property, which is about half the size of New York's Central Park. Two-hundred-foot sycamores tower above the slate roof of the stone main house. Acres of lawns, stone walls, manicured flower beds, and an

English walled garden extend to the edge of the forest. Guests can stay in the main building, at the Century Farm House, or the Garden House.

When you come for a weekend there are never more than twenty-five other couples. All meals and an open bar are included in the price as is use of the indoor and outdoor swimming pools, whirlpool and sauna, tennis courts, and exercise equipment.

The rooms are all individually decorated; four have working fireplaces. Generous common space on the first floor of the main inn includes a conference room, large living room, library, and a couple of smaller rooms, all of which are open to guests. The guest rooms are on the second and third floors of this rambling mansion. The Century Farm House is one large building with eighteen rooms. Part of it is 240 years old and part is brand new. In the middle there is a large living room. The Garden House has three large bedrooms; guests share the living room and kitchen. The two second-floor rooms have decks that overlook the walled garden, and the first-floor room has a patio.

There are two dining rooms that overlook the gardens. A five-course dinner that allows guests to choose from the menu is included for overnight guests. A sampling of items from a recent menu included appetizers of capellini with smoked chicken breast, oyster mushrooms, and artichoke hearts; canellini beans with tasso ham and tomato; and grilled sea scallops with grilled pineapples and mango salsa. Entrées included oat-crusted halibut filet, grilled veal chop with fresh chanterelles and roasted shallots, grilled swordfish steak with sun-dried tomato sauce and guacamole, and grilled tenderloin of beef with champagne-mustard vinaigrette. Desserts featured Grand Marnier, peach, and almond soufflés; a chocolate ganache tarte; lemon curd in a cookie tulip; and several flavors of homemade gelato.

Thirty-four rooms and suites, thirty-two with private bath, $375–$475 including three meals and spirits for Friday or Saturday night; $575–$790 for Friday and Saturday nights, all meals

and spirits. 12% service charge. Children over 12 welcome. No
pets. Dinner on Friday and Saturday, 6:30 to 9 P.M. Entrées,
$16.95–$23.50; five-course prix fixe dinner, $39.50. Sunday
brunch, 11:30 A.M. to 1:30 P.M.; $26 includes wine. Off Route
343 between Amenia and Sharon. Leedsville Road, Amenia, NY
12501; (914) 373-9681.

What to Do.   If you decide to leave this magnificent setting
(many couples don't) you can visit the galleries in Kent, or the
Eric Sloane museum, which features the artist's paintings and
his early-American tool collection. Kent Falls State Park has a
path that follows a 200-foot waterfall. The area is full of antique
shops. West Cornwall has a beautiful one-lane covered bridge
over the Housatonic River. Drive to Salisbury, another lovely
small New England town, for excellent tea and cake at Chaiwalla
Tea Room.

How to Get There.   From New York get on I-684 north
to Brewster. Continue on Route 22 north to Amenia. Turn right
on Route 343 east toward Sharon. Go 2.4 miles to the sign.

JANE STAUFFER

Old Drovers Inn, *Dover Plains, New York*

Almost 250 years of continuous use have imparted a warm glow of welcome to this historic inn. The dark, low-ceilinged, wood-beamed taproom with its great stone fireplace is one of the coziest and most intimate dining spots we've seen. Four gracious guest rooms invite travelers to stop and rest.

Innkeepers Alice Pitcher and Kemper Peacock have admirably preserved this museum-quality gem, which was just admitted to the Relais and Chateaux international association of deluxe inns. On the first floor there is a formal library, a parlor with an antique bird cage housing zebra finches, and a front-hall lounge with a wood-burning fireplace and a down-filled couch. Notice the antique chest whose legs had to be drastically altered to compensate for the sagging floor. The building reminds us of an elderly aristocratic lady whose slight idiosyncrasies have become part of her charm.

For a winter stay our choices are the three rooms with wood-burning fireplaces. Our favorite is the largest and the most sumptuous, the Meeting Room with two double beds, a barrel-shaped ceiling, and two wing chairs set in front of a wood-burning fireplace. The other rooms with fireplaces are the Cherry Room with two double beds and the Sleigh Room with a double sleigh bed. Nice touches include the thick terrycloth robes and the evening turndown service accompanied by an apple, chocolate thin mints, chocolate truffles, and ice water.

Juice and freshly brewed coffee are set out for early-rising guests in the first-floor Federal Room, where breakfast is served beginning at 9 A.M. The walls of this room are decorated with murals painted in 1941 of the inn, West Point, and Hyde Park. Start breakfast with a glass of freshly squeezed orange or grapefruit juice and homemade breakfast breads. On the weekends this is followed by a choice of omelets with wild mushrooms or cheddar cheese, French toast baguette, Belgian malted waffles, shepherd's eggs on hash browns, or Southern-style grits, all served with breakfast meats.

Both lunch and dinner are served to inn guests and the general public in the taproom. Lighting is supplied mainly by candles set inside etched hurricane lamps, and from reflections cast by teapots and bottles arranged on a recessed shelf around the dining room.

Traditions of the inn include double-size drinks served in hand-blown crystal glasses, accompanied by stuffed eggs, a bowl of crudités, and a specially made hickory-smoked salt.

The blackboard menu is hung on hooks by your table. Cheddar cheese soup is always on the menu, as is browned turkey hash. The lobster hash recipe served with a Benedictine and brandy corn sauce recently won a national contest. The lamb chops are exceptional. We like the option of ordering one or two double-thick chops trimmed of excess fat, perfectly grilled, and served with tomato chutney. Smoked pork chops come from the Egg and I, a local farm, and are served with a spicy black-and-white-bean salad. Other house specialties are breast of Muscovy duck and Black Angus cowboy steak. Piping hot popovers accompany the entrées . . . always a treat.

For dessert we liked the peppermint-stick-candy ice cream, specially made for Old Drovers, and served with hot fudge sauce, or traditional favorites such as pecan or key lime pie, or crème brûlée.

Four rooms, all with private bath, $110–$170. Midweek, $100–$150. 10% service charge. Country breakfast included on the weekends, continental breakfast midweek. Children and pets permitted with advance notice, additional fee.

Lunch Thursday through Saturday, 12 to 3 P.M., $10–$20. Sunday brunch, 12 to 2 P.M., $11.50–$13.50. Dinner Monday and Thursday, 5:30 to 9 P.M.; Friday, to 9:30 P.M.; Saturday, 3 to 10 P.M.; Sunday, 2 to 8:30 P.M. Entrées, $16.50–$31. 20% gratuity added to the bill. Off Route 22. Old Drovers Road, Dover Plains, NY 12522; (914) 832-9311.

What to Do. The inn is ideally situated for day trips in a number of different directions. An hour to the west is Hyde Park, home of the Franklin Delano Roosevelt National Historic Site, the grand Italian Renaissance Vanderbilt Mansion, and the Culinary Institute of America, where you can have a superb meal prepared by America's top young chefs. Take a cruise or a sail on the Hudson River. Horseback riding is available in nearby Millerton at Western Riding Stables. The Appalachian Trail crosses nearby. Head east across Bull's Bridge into Connecticut's Litchfield County. There you can visit the galleries in Kent or the Eric Sloane museum featuring the artist and writer's paintings and his early American tool collection. Take the path at Kent Falls State Park that follows the 200-foot waterfall. The area is full of antique shops and old bookstores. West Cornwall has a beautiful one-lane covered bridge over the Housatonic River and the workshop of Ian Ingersoll, one of the best handcrafted furniture makers in New England, with Shaker reproductions his specialty. Drive to New Preston and have a look at a dozen or so upscale antique stores and drive around beautiful Lake Waramaug. Canoe or fly-fish the Housatonic River.

How to Get There.   From New York City, take I-684 north to Brewster. Take Route 22 north. The inn is located just off Route 22 (on Old Route 22) between Wingdale and Dover Plains.

The Delamater House at Beekman Arms

Beekman Arms, *Rhinebeck, New York*

Travelers have been stopping for food and lodging at this centrally located inn in the Hudson River valley for 226 years. There are a wide variety of rooms, many with wood-burning fireplaces, located in ten buildings, all within a block of the main building. The front entrance lobby where guests check in is particularly welcoming on a cold day with an old stone fireplace surrounded by easy chairs and a high-backed bench. The most important change since our previous visits is that Larry Forgione, one of America's most talented chefs and owner of An American Place restaurant in New York City, has taken over the management of the Beekman Arms restaurant.

Our favorite fireplace accommodation is suite 90, a quiet second-floor apartment with its own entrance. In the large living room with a fireplace, sofa, easy chairs, and table we were happy to spend the day curled up in front of the fireplace, reading the books we'd brought along. The kitchen is fully equipped with a toaster, microwave oven, and a refrigerator stocked with sodas and a few snack foods. The bedroom is relatively small with a queen-size brass bed.

If a fireplace is not a priority, our favorite accommodation is room 52 in the Delamater House, a magnificent 1844 American Gothic building that drips with gingerbread trim. Room 52, along with the foyer and sitting room on the first floor, were decorated by the New York firm of Brunschwig & Fils using their designer fabrics. The room has high ceilings; a queen-size four-poster bed with matching curtains, wallpaper, and pillows on the wicker chairs and sofa; a bay window; and a bath with a shower only. The building is located close to the main street in Rhinebeck; if traffic noise bothers you, stay in the Delamater Courtyard instead.

The sixteen Delamater Courtyard rooms each have a wood-burning fireplace, a television hidden in an armoire, a queen-size bed or two double beds, and a large desk in the bedroom. Rooms 80 through 83 are similar to the Courtyard rooms but also include kitchenettes with refrigerators and microwave ovens. The Gables, a Victorian house located next to the Delamater House, has four rooms with reproduction antiques. It is designated for non-smoking adults only. Room 84, across the hall from the parlor, has a queen-size pencil-post bed, a television tucked into the armoire, and a large bath that also includes a bidet.

Other accommodations include a one-story Guest House motel, not our choice; two large rooms with steep staircases located over what was once the firehouse; and rooms on the second and third floors of the main inn. We do like the traditional country-inn character of the rooms in the main inn, which include a pants press, a unique touch. However, we suggest that you inquire about the specifics of these rooms; most do not have televisions or air-conditioning, and some are located in sections of the inn where the noise from the street, dining room, or taproom could be disturbing.

Sophisticated American cuisine is chef Larry Forgione's trademark. Among his specialties are a delicate summer-squash and sweet-corn soup with red-pepper cream, and crab and sweet-corn griddle cakes. The night we dined we had an elegantly presented appetizer of crisp gaufrettes of potatoes layered with slivers of smoked salmon and a dab of lemon cream and tender fried calamari served with spicy rémoulade sauce. Perch cooked on a cedar plank was served on a bed of sweet potato and corn pudding. The fish was cooked on the rare side, which our waiter told us was intentional. A stew of mild smoked bay scallops, white beans with fusilli pasta, roasted garlic, oregano, and bacon served with a warm loaf of dark sourdough bread was enough for a meal. For chocoholics we suggest the moist, dense chocolate-fudge cake with pecans and espresso sauce.

Fifty-nine rooms and suites, all with private bath, $70–$110; suite 90, $140. Two-night minimum on weekends from mid-May through October and holiday weekends. Continental breakfast provided for guests staying at the Delamater House, the Carriage House, the Gables, and the Courtyard rooms. Breakfast buffet available at the inn for an additional charge. Children welcome except in the Delamater House and the Gables. Pets welcome in the motel-style rooms only. The dining room is open daily for breakfast, lunch, and dinner. Lunch, 11:30 A.M. to 3

P.M., $5.95–$12.95. Dinner, 5:30 P.M. to 9 or 10 P.M.; entrées, $12.95–$22.95. Sunday brunch, 10 A.M. to 2 P.M., $19.95. Route 9, Rhinebeck, NY 12572; (914) 876–7077.

What to Do. The work of the great nineteenth-century romantic landscape painters who came to be known as the Hudson River School—Asher B. Durand, Thomas Cole, John Kensett, Jasper Cropsey, Frederick Church, and others—made this area of the United States famous. Visit Olana, Frederick Church's home in Hudson. Cross the river and drive west to Kaaterskill Falls along Route 23A and to the site of the Catskill Mountain House in North Lake State Park for one of the greatest panoramic views of the Hudson River valley. Play the Red Baron by taking a ride in an old biplane at the Rhinebeck Aerodrome, a living museum of antique aircraft.

Visit the opulent Vanderbilt Mansion and Franklin D. Roosevelt's home and library in Hyde Park. Have lunch or dinner at one of the four restaurants at the Culinary Institute of America in West Point, where tomorrow's great chefs are in training. Take a cruise on the Hudson River from Kingston Rondout Landing to fully experience this valley and especially to see the grand old estates.

In Garrison-on-Hudson visit Boscobel, a meticulously restored and maintained Federal mansion filled with an outstanding collection of New York Federal furniture. The front porch of Boscobel has a breathtaking view of the Hudson River.

How to Get There. From New York City, take the Taconic State Parkway north. Head west on Route 308 to Route 9. Or take I-87 north to Kingston, east on Route 199, south on Route 9 to the inn.

The Spa Suite

Inn New York City, *New York, New York*

Located less than a block from the excitement of Broadway, the main street and spinal cord of New York's Upper West Side residential district (north of the theatrical mecca) is one of the most intimate, romantic, quiet, and eclectic accommodations in the city of cities.

You'll be greeted by owners Elyn and Ruth Mensch, longtime residents of the West Side, who renovated and furnished the four spacious luxurious country-style suites in this classic late-nineteenth-century brownstone on West Seventy-first Street.

Each suite has a fully equipped kitchen stocked with breakfast items and snacks such as bagels, quiche, pancake mix, muffins, scones, crackers, maple syrup, jam, juices, sodas, tea, fresh ground coffee, and a bottle of wine. Each suite has a telephone with a private number and an answering machine that you can program with a message. All of the suites have a television and a stereo tape deck; three suites also have washer/dryers.

Ruth and Elyn, a mother and daughter team, cater to individual needs and special requests. One regular guest, a leading tenor who appears at the Metropolitan Opera several times a season, likes candy bars and cookies, so his suite is stocked with them before he arrives. One guest wanted a romantic afternoon for herself and her beau; the Mensches arranged for a violinist to play in the hallway outside the suite. For a couple who arrived by horse-drawn carriage from their wedding reception, they arranged to have the couple's suite filled with bouquets of red roses.

Our favorite accommodation is the second-floor Spa Suite. A king-size bed sits on a raised platform. There is an antique chestnut armoire, a closet that opens to reveal a television, stereo system, and an extensive collection of books and magazines. Almost half of the suite is a spa complete with sauna, shower, bidet, and a large double Jacuzzi that sits majestically in the middle of the room. An old barber chair stands in one corner and glass block windows let in filtered light.

The Loft Suite on the third floor has an airy country feeling. The living room has a fourteen-foot beamed ceiling; an exposed brick wall decorated with baskets, old dolls, children's chairs, and other collectibles; an English Chesterfield leather sofa that converts to a queen-size bed; a leaded stained-glass skylight; and a wood-burning fireplace. A separate orange sponge-painted bedroom has a queen-size bed with a leaded stained-glass skylight overhead. The small bathroom has a marble and brass sink.

The first-floor Parlor Suite, which is more than fifty feet long with a twelve-foot ceiling, has an elegant formal look. At one end is a raised platform furnished with an oval dining-room table in front of the window, a Baldwin spinet piano, and a chaise longue. At the other end of the living-room suite, closet doors open to reveal a queen-size Murphy bed that faces a wood-burning fireplace. There is a stained-glass window over the center kitchen area. The bath has a single Jacuzzi.

The Vermont Suite on the ground floor has its own private entrance. The living room has a contemporary country decor with an oak and pine convertible couch, a platform rocker, and a fully equipped kitchen with a tile floor. A steep Victorian spiral iron staircase leads to the lower level, where there is a bedroom with a queen-size bed and a headboard made from an old iron gate.

This inn has no sign in front, so only those who know where they are going will ever find this special, almost-secret romantic hideaway.

Four suites: Vermont Suite, $175; Loft Suite, $195; Spa Suite, $225; Parlor Suite, $240. Each additional person, $35. At most times there is a two-night minimum; $25 surcharge for arrivals after 10 P.M. Not appropriate for children. No pets. 19.25% city and state tax and $2 occupancy tax is additional. 266 West Seventy-first Street, New York, NY 10023; (212) 580-1900.

Where to Dine. Check with Elyn or Ruth for the new restaurants in the area. For brunch, Sarabeth's Kitchen on Amsterdam Avenue at Eightieth Street (212-496-6280) is a popular choice. Arrive before 10 A.M. on Saturday or you'll have to wait in line. We like the beautiful, classy Café des Artistes (1 West Sixty-seventh Street; 212-877-3500) better for brunch; the walls feature the famous Christy nude murals. The intimate bar is also a favorite. The place to see and be seen on the West Side is Café Luxembourg at 200 West Seventieth Street (212-873-7411). Its noisy 1930s Paris atmosphere includes a zinc bar and mirrored walls. Stop at Café La Fortuna on West Seventy-first Street off Columbus Avenue, for cappuccino, dessert, and great operas on the stereo. Andiamo is a spacious, contemporary art-filled restaurant with excellent Northern Italian food on Broadway and

Sixty-eighth Street on the second floor (212-362-3315). It is behind Il Bel Canto, a public space where you can brown-bag it or get a light bite. Gray's Papaya, a stand-up counter on the southeast corner of Seventy-second and Broadway, has the best buy in the city—two grilled hotdogs with sauerkraut and mustard and a papaya drink for $2.

What to Do.   The Upper West Side is home to many of New York's writers, actors, and musicians. It extends from the Hudson River to Central Park and from Columbus Circle at Fifty-ninth Street to Columbia University at 114th Street. A highlight of the area is Lincoln Center for the Performing Arts, a grand complex from Sixty-second to Sixty-fifth streets and Columbus Avenue. Notice the pair of Chagall murals at the entrance to the Metropolitan Opera House. Get tickets to see a performance or take a tour.

Window-shop your way up Columbus Avenue, which is filled with fashionable boutiques, to the Museum of Natural History at Seventy-seventh Street, and Central Park West. Tasting our way along the west side of Broadway is a favorite pastime. Fairway market at Seventy-fourth Street, is renowned for its cheese, wild mushrooms, and breads. Stop at Citarella's Fish Market (Seventy-fifth Street), to look at the window display; H&H Bagels (Seventy-ninth Street) where 70,000 bagels are made each day; Zabar's (Eightieth Street) to buy salmon, prepared foods, cheeses, coffee, bread, or to visit the second-floor shop for discounted cookware; and Murray's Sturgeon (Eighty-ninth Street), an old-fashioned smoked-fish shop where the herring with onions and cream is ambrosia.

Rose Inn, *Ithaca, New York*

Innkeepers Charles and Sherry Rosemann are consummate professionals. Unlike many other innkeepers, Charles was trained in hotel-management schools in Germany and managed five-star hotels in the United States before joining Sherry to run their own inn. Their teamwork, attention to detail, and constant striving for perfection is most commendable.

For a romantic getaway, what could be better than a spacious, luxuriously appointed room with a Jacuzzi big enough for two and dinner in a private dining room? Of the three rooms with Jacuzzis at the Rose Inn, the ultimate is the bridal suite, which has a double Jacuzzi surrounded by fan-shaped Palladian windows overlooking the gardens, a stand of white pines, a fifty-year-old apple orchard, and fields of corn beyond. The fireplace is visible from the king-size bed, the Eames chair, or the love seat.

A ground-floor suite has a living room with French doors leading to a flower garden. The king-size bed is in the same room but gives the impression of greater privacy, as it's on a level four steps higher than the rest of the room. The large bath has a double Jacuzzi and a separate shower. Note the eighteen-inch-tall carved white falcon: the United States Air Force Academy liked this model of its mascot so much that it commissioned a duplicate.

The third room with a double Jacuzzi has a skylight, king-size bed with an ornate brass headboard, and an old-fashioned, large white porcelain sink. On a slightly smaller scale are twelve additional well-decorated rooms clustered around two sitting areas where the telephones are located. One of the sitting areas has a refrigerator stocked with wines and champagne. Out-of-the-ordinary amenities in the rooms include French soap and other toiletries, thick bath sheets, terrycloth robes, adjustable shower heads, and padded satin hangers.

After you're thoroughly relaxed, dress for dinner and descend the Honduran-mahogany circular staircase—the centerpiece of this 1850s Italianate mansion that sits, along with several classic eighteenth-century barns, on twenty acres of photogenic farmland just outside of Ithaca.

If you appreciate fine dining, this is an experience you should not miss. "Do a Few Things Perfectly" is the motto that Charles and Sherry strictly adhere to as they plan their dinner selections. The policy at this country inn is for guests to select their appetizer and entrée before arriving for dinner. Diners are seated in the center hall, in the parlor, or in one of two intimate dining rooms. Fine linens, fresh flowers, candles, china, and silver flatware frame your meal.

As a first course, try the sinfully rich, richly flavored lobster bisque made with chunks of lobster and heavy cream. The artichoke-heart strudel served on puréed tomato is also excellent and somewhat lighter than the bisque. A third delectable appetizer is the smoked oysters in beurre blanc sauce served in a flaky puff-pastry shell. The salad, one of the best we've had, is an artistic presentation that includes Boston lettuce, radicchio, artichoke hearts, hearts of palm, red and yellow peppers, tomatoes, and sprouts.

If you like duck tender with no excess fat, it is always available here by special request. The grilled rack of lamb, veal chops, and fish dishes are cooked outdoors year-round on charcoal grills. The veal chop is served with a classic Madeira sauce and topped with sliced, sautéed wild mushrooms. The lamb chops are marinated in garlic and herbs. The scampi is sautéed with tomato, curry, and cream, and flambéed with brandy. The colorful combination of steamed broccoli, cauliflower, and slivered carrots artfully arranged in a crisp potato basket is the ultimate vegetable dish. The small, thoroughly researched, reasonably priced wine list is designed to complement the entrées. Dessert may be a rich chocolate pot de crème or a cornucopia-shaped *pizzelle* filled with locally grown raspberries set on crème Anglaise.

This attention to elegant detail continues at breakfast. You may start with a mixture of freshly squeezed Israeli blood oranges and California Valencias. During the fall season, enjoy a glass of apple cider made from the inn's apples. The coffee is a mixture of Kona, Colombian, and Amaretto. A fruit dish might include raspberries and blueberries served with crème fraîche and brown sugar. A breakfast entrée could be salmon arranged in the shape of a rose, served with bagels and cream cheese, or German apple pancakes served with the inn's own apple butter.

Twelve rooms, all with private bath, $100–$150; three suites all with a Jacuzzi for two, $175–$250. Full breakfast included. Two-night minimum stay on weekends. Children over 10 welcome. Third person in room $25 additional. No pets. Dinner served Tuesday through Saturday at 7 P.M.; 24-hour advance reservations required; $50 per person prix fixe. On Route 34, nine miles north of the city. 813 Auburn Road, Route 34, Box 6576, Ithaca, NY 14851-6576; (607) 533-7905.

What to Do. Six long narrow lakes named for the Indians who inhabited the region (Cayuga, Seneca, Skaneateles, Owasco,

Keuka, and Canandaigua) lie side by side, ranging in length from eleven to forty miles and varying in depth from 177 to more than 600 feet. These six finger lakes span a distance of sixty miles. Four smaller lakes lie slightly farther to the west. All the major lakes have cruises that operate from mid-May to mid-September. At the southern edges of the lakes, the land is studded with miles of easily accessible, well-maintained trails that follow the deep gorges and breathtaking waterfalls. Along the hillsides of the lakes are miles of vineyards. Between the lakes are colorful valleys of rolling farmland where dairy herds are raised and buckwheat and fruits are grown.

At the Corning Glass Center you can see Steuben pieces hand-blown and engraved. The Museum of Glass exhibits pieces of glass ranging in age from 2,000 years to contemporary. Cornell University, set on a hill overlooking Lake Cayuga, is worth a visit. Stop in at the famous Moosewood vegetarian restaurant in Ithaca, which is still owned and operated by a cooperative of eighteen members. Walk along the gorges in nearby Buttermilk Falls State Park, Taughannock Falls State Park, or Robert Tremain State Park. More than forty wineries now operate in the Finger Lakes region. The white wines, especially the Chardonnays and Rieslings, are worth tasting. Hermann Wiemer, Wagner, and Bully Hill are interesting vineyards to visit.

How to Get There. From New York City, take I-87 north to I-84 west. When you reach Scranton, take I-81 north to Cortland, Route 13 to Ithaca, and Route 34 north to the inn.

JANE STAUFFER

The Whitehall Inn, *New Hope, Pennsylvania*

The grandfather clock chimed nine. The two tables, covered with white linen, were set with stemmed glasses, Villeroy and Boch flower-pattern china, and ornate Victorian sterling flatware. Lighted tapers glowed on the tables; side buffets were bright with candles of varying heights and pots of red poinsettias. Sunlight sparkled through the seventy-seven panes of the large window overlooking the Bucks County countryside. What followed was an extraordinary one-and-a-half-hour breakfast.

Beverage Course

Whitehall's Special Blend of Coffee
Selection of Thirty English and Herbal Teas
Freshly Squeezed Honey Tangerine Juice

Bread Course

*Cinnamon Streusel Coffee Cake
Raised Buckwheat Biscuits Served with
Raspberry Jam and Butter*

Soup Course

Chilled Peach and Sherry Soup

Fruit Course

Cinnamon-Crusted Baked Pear with a Cognac Custard Sauce

Main Course

Spinach Tarts with Toasted Pine Nuts and Parmesan Cheese

An Appropriate Ending

Whitehall Chocolate

Go ahead, indulge yourself—you only live once! We savored this breakfast on a cold January morning. Innkeepers Mike and Suella Wass beautifully orchestrated the meal: Suella baked, sautéed, and souffléed in the kitchen while Mike elegantly served and chatted with the guests. Each morning the menu is different. In fact, the Wasses keep your menus on file so that you'll never get a repeat on subsequent visits (unless you make a special request).

When you return to the inn at 4 P.M., the aromas of Suella's baking and freshly brewed tea make you forget that you resolved not to eat another thing all day. Sitting by the fire on a recent visit, we enthusiastically sampled peach tea, orange and currant scones, ginger-cream sandwiches, chocolate cookies, and red grapes.

The living room is warm and inviting: furnishings include comfortable couches, rocking chairs (including original Shaker chairs), Oriental carpets, a wood-burning fireplace, sconces with lighted candles, and Suella's fine needlepoint samplers. Guests can also sit in the plant-filled enclosed entrance porch and try their hand at one of the half-finished puzzles.

For a romantic stay, we recommend the Albert Hibbs Room. The queen-size bed has lacy, ecru-colored, 200-thread-count hand-ironed sheets. There are at least six pillows on each bed, and so you can have firm pillows for reading and choose between down and Quallofil for sleeping. Slip into the velour robes provided by the inn, light the fire, and open the bottle of Vidal Blanc (from nearby Buckingham Vineyards). The large bath is thoughtfully stocked with Ralph Lauren towels, Crabtree & Evelyn colognes, talcum powder, shampoo, conditioner, and custom-blended bath salts, plus a selection of individually wrapped soaps. At night, when your bed is turned down, two handmade truffles imprinted with a Whitehall "W" are placed on your pillow.

Next to the Albert Hibbs is the equally spacious Gerald Gimsey Room with Williamsburg potpourri wallpaper, a fireplace, and a queen-size bed made with lacy sheets. This room shares a bath with one other room. All of Whitehall's guests are pampered with a bottle of wine, truffles, bath soaps, and colognes.

The smaller Phineas Kelly Room is popular, as it is adjacent to the living room. In the late evening, guests like to curl up in front of the wood-burning fireplace.

In warmer weather, guests spend time relaxing around the outdoor swimming pool, playing tennis, and feeding the horses. You'll discover thoughtful touches throughout your stay: flannel sheets in winter, sherry in the evening, a personal note when you leave. And if you return, there's always a surprise in store for you.

Five rooms; three with private bath, two with fireplaces.

Weekends, $130–$170, midweek, $110–$160. Four of the rooms have fireplaces. Gourmet breakfast and afternoon tea included. Two-night minimum stay on weekends. Children over 12 welcome. No pets. No smoking. RD 2, Box 250, Pineville Road, New Hope, PA 18938; (215) 598-7945.

Special Theme Weekends:

Presidents' Day Weekend. Celebrates Valentine's Day too and includes a special romantic breakfast.

Chocolate Lovers' Weekend. Includes a chocolate high tea, chamber music, chocolate breakfast, and a talk by a chocolate expert. Held the weekend after Easter.

Baroque Tea Concert. Quartet performs baroque music at an afternoon high tea in the middle of May.

Holiday Picnic Weekends. Memorial Day, Independence Day, and Labor Day. Great picnics are served on the grounds.

Strawberry High Tea. Chamber music followed by high tea. First weekend in June.

Champagne Candlelight Concert. Chamber music, champagne, and hors d'oeuvres. New Year's Eve.

Where to Dine.   The finest and most expensive classic French dining is at La Bonne Auberge in New Hope (Village 2; 215-862-2462). A favorite entrée is a large lobster tail filled with chunks of lobster meat combined with mushrooms, pimiento, cheeses, and a champagne sauce.

In Lambertville, New Jersey (just across the Delaware River), Anton's at the Swan (42 South Main Street; 609-397-1960) changes the menu monthly. Recent appetizers include grilled scallops over pumpkin risotto or grilled sweetbreads with a wild mushroom and lentil purée, with entrées of roast pheasant with sage and pork stuffing or roast halibut with sorrel. For a lighter meal, go to Hamilton's Grill in Lambertville (8½ Coryell

Street; 609-397-4343). If you are here on a Friday, Saturday, or Sunday night, reserve a table for an elegant, prix-fixe, seven-course dinner at EverMay on the Delaware in Erwinna, about 25 minutes north of New Hope on Route 32 (215-294-9100). Call ahead to see if the menu appeals, as dinner includes a choice of two entrées and two desserts.

What to Do. Galleries and shops are just minutes away in New Hope, Lambertville, and Peddler's Village. At the fascinating Mercer Museum in Doylestown you can see an amazing hodgepodge of tools and crafts from more than sixty trades, all dating from before 1850. A conglomeration of items, including a Conestoga wagon and a whaling boat, are suspended from the six-story atrium ceiling.

Outdoor enthusiasts can hike or bike along the Delaware Canal towpath, which is sixty miles long. Explore New Hope, a 300-year-old artists' community. Rice's Market near New Hope, open Tuesday from 7 A.M. to noon, is a bargain hunter's delight with stalls selling everything from antiques and collectibles to sheets, clothing, furs, and wallpaper. Antiquers will want to tour the dozens of antique shops along Route 202 in Pennsylvania between New Hope and Lahaska. In the summer, you can rent tubes for a leisurely float down the Delaware River or take a mule-drawn barge ride on the canal.

How to Get There. From Philadelphia take I-95 north to Newtown exit, Route 332 west to Newtown. Take Route 413 north to Pineville. Turn right at the Pineville Tavern on Pineville Road.

From New York, take the New Jersey Turnpike south to exit 10, Route 287 north to Route 22 west, and Route 202 south to Lahaska. Turn left on Street Road. Turn right on Stoney Hill Road. Turn left on Pineville Road.

JANE STAUFFER

Sweetwater Farm, *Glen Mills, Pennsylvania*

Turning in the circular drive, off a narrow country road dotted with private estates, we arrived at a large eighteenth-century fieldstone manor house. A flag fluttered above the front door; the brick walkway was lined with bright flowers; graceful, majestic trees told us that skilled arborists had been at work. Sweetwater is far more than an elegant inn: along with cottages and a swimming pool, it is a fifty-acre farm with sheep and horses grazing in the fields. This idyllic retreat in Pennsylvania's Brandywine River valley (made famous by Andrew Wyeth's paintings) epitomizes the gentleman farmer's domain. The current resident innkeeper is Barbara Pietsch.

The library, with its wall of books, is a comfortably casual room where guests can sit by the fireplace engrossed in the Sunday papers. Across the hall there is a sunny formal parlor. In warm weather, the terrace overlooking the fields and swimming pool is a favorite spot.

There are number of cottages on the property. The Green-house Cottage, created from the former greenhouse, is the best cottage. It has two bedrooms (the bath is off one of the bedrooms), a full kitchen, a living room with a fireplace, a washer/dryer, and a private patio. We would not select this cottage for a visit in the middle of the summer, as the large number of windows puts a greater strain on the air-conditioning unit. The Gardener's Cottage has a bedroom with a queen-size canopy bed and a sitting room with a fireplace. The Windowbox Cottage has a bedroom with a double bed, a kitchen, living room, a bath with a shower only, and a washer and dryer. One drawback to the cottages is that they are near the barn, where large horse trailers come and go at night. If you are a light sleeper we suggest staying in the main inn.

The Fan-window Suite on the third floor is a favorite with honeymooners. The wallpaper is white with pink roses: white plaster walls, white wicker couches, white chairs, and a white headboard for the queen-size bed. The small bathroom has a white clawfoot tub.

Across the hall is the Loft Room, which has a queen-size and a double bed. This room reminds us of Wyeth paintings, with dark woods, a large spinning wheel, skeins of yarn in a basket, and a staircase that once led to the attic but now is purely decorative. In contrast to the bath in the Fan-window Suite, this one is large and modern.

We like the Lafayette Room, the only room in the main inn with a fireplace, a queen-size canopy bed, and a private bath (shower only). For those on a budget who want the romance of a fireplace room and don't mind sharing a bath, the Georgian Room on the second floor fits the bill. The room has large windows and a high four-poster queen-size bed with a fishnet canopy. This room shares a large hall bath with the Master Bedroom and the Nursery Room.

Breakfast, served in the country kitchen, includes fresh eggs, country sausage, fresh fruit, juice, homemade breads such as bran muffins or cinnamon rolls, and cereals.

One could easily spend the entire day without leaving the property—at the swimming pool, sitting under the large trees, and enjoying the vast open space outdoors. Be aware, however, that there is an active quarry (audible but not oppressively so) beyond the trees.

Six rooms and four cottages with private bath, $145–$225. Three rooms with shared bath, $145. Country breakfast included. There are phones in all and televisions in most of the rooms. Children welcome. Third person in room, $25 additional. Small dogs permitted in the cottages. 50 Sweetwater Road, Glen Mills, PA 19342; (215) 459-4711.

Where to Dine.   On a Friday or Saturday night, visit Wilmington, Delaware, a thirty-minute drive, and dine in elegance in the exquisite Green Room at the Hotel du Pont (Eleventh and Market Streets; 302-594-3154). Recently refurbished to its original 1913 elegance, it is on par with the world's great hotel dining rooms. Elaborate dinners are prepared in the French continental style, such as a delicate seafood sausage in white wine sauce with chunks of Maine lobster (for an American touch) and truffles. A harpist serenades guests from a balcony box.

The closest restaurant to Sweetwater Farm is Pace One, located in a restored 1740s stone barn (Thornton and Glen Mills Road, Thornton; 215-459-3702). On the night we dined, the mixed grill combined baby lamb chops, venison sausage, and quail, accompanied by apple chutney. For romantic dining we suggest the candlelit Dilworthtown Inn (Old Wilmington Pike, West Chester; 215-399-1390). The 1758 stone building has thirteen dining rooms on three floors, many with only five tables. Since this area is the mushroom-growing capital of the United States, the restaurant has two mushroom appetizers: a medley of wild mushrooms sautéed with Chartreuse and sherry, and wild-mushroom pasta in a vodka cream sauce. For a casual lunch of traditional diner fare, try Hank's Place across the street from the Brandywine River Museum (Route 1, Chadds Ford).

What to Do. The 350 acres of magnificent Longwood Gardens, located on Route 1 three miles east of Kennett Square, should not be missed. There is an Italian water garden, rock garden, vegetable, perennial, and wildflower gardens, along with illuminated fountain displays, a bell tower, eye of water, and four acres of stunning, landscaped conservatories. The flowers and plants in the great open areas of the conservatory are changed frequently throughout the year.

The Winterthur mansion is the country's premier museum of American decorative arts: 83,000 objects are on display in nearly 200 room settings dating from periods covering 1640 to 1840. Take one of the reserved tours, usually of no more than four persons, led by a knowledgeable, highly trained guide.

The Brandywine River Museum, a restored nineteenth-century gristmill on the banks of the Brandywine River, is home to three generations of Wyeth paintings, which are on permanent display. The third-floor Andrew Wyeth gallery exhibits approximately forty watercolors, dry brush, and tempera paintings that represent Andrew Wyeth's career from 1938 to the present.

How to Get There. From New York, take the New Jersey Turnpike south to exit 2. Take Route 322 west. Go north, a right turn, on Route 452. Turn left and drive one mile on Route 1. Turn right at Valley Road (Franklin Mint intersection). At the end of the road, turn left and immediately right. Continue three quarters of a mile to Sweetwater Road. Turn left and drive for half a mile to the farm.

From Washington, D.C., take I-95 north to Wilmington. Take Route 202 north to Route 1. Turn right on Route 1 for five miles to Valley Road. Then follow the preceding directions.

The Gold Room

Smithton Inn, *Ephrata, Pennsylvania*

Candlelight danced on the walls of our room. Flames flickered in the fireplace. The full-length canopy draped gently around the edges of the bed. Chamber music played softly in the background. After soaking in the whirlpool, we donned the flannel nightshirts that are put in each room and slipped into the caressing comfort of the featherbed. Propped up with down pillows and covered with a locally made quilt, we felt utterly pampered.

This was our introduction to Smithton, located in the heart of Lancaster County, Pennsylvania, home of the Amish. Here you can combine a stay in a romantic hideaway with a look at an authentic early American lifestyle as practiced by the Plain People of Lancaster County.

Innkeeper Dorothy Graybill, along with partner Allan Smith, lavish attention on the impeccable details of this 1763 stone house. They have incorporated numerous decorative influences from the nearby Ephrata Cloister into the design of the inn. On display in the living room is an original copy of *Martyrs Mirror*

(1,200 pages), the largest book published in Colonial America, which was printed at the Ephrata Cloister. Notice the Cloister-inspired wooden door hinges, the hand-planed floors, the hand-crafted dining room buffet, and the inn's emblem of two doves on the quilt and carved headboard in the Gold Room.

The accommodation of choice is the South Wing Suite, actually a small duplex apartment, which is a study tour of eighteenth-century furnishings. Enter through the authentic "Indian door" (designed with a sliding wooden panel to protect settlers from Indian attacks). The first floor has a living room with black leather sofas, leather wing chairs, and a fireplace. The kitchen is stocked with cold sodas, juice, and snacks for nibbling. Off the kitchen there is a small screened porch. Upstairs, the queen-size bed is made with one of the most beautiful Amish quilts we have seen: a meticulously detailed tree-of-life pattern. Encasing the head of the bed are fine hand-woven blue hangings. An enclosed twin Dutch bed constructed with wooden pegs provides an unusual sleeping alternative. A large bathroom features a stall shower as well as a whirlpool tub.

Another favorite of ours, secluded at the back of the inn, is the Gold Room. Gold velvet draperies match the full canopy of the queen-size bed. The colorful quilt and the tin and copper cut-out lampshades were inspired by Ephrata Cloister drawings. Notice the hand-painted blanket chest, the gleaming hand-pounded copper sink, the black leather chairs, and the fireplace strategically situated at the foot of the bed.

The White Room on the third floor, with exposed beams, a slanted ceiling with skylights, and a wood stove, is popular with guests who want a large, private loft space in which to hibernate. This room has a queen-size rope bed. The bath has a clawfoot tub, but no shower.

There are four rooms on the second floor. The Red Room, with a double bed, has a step-up whirlpool tub with a hand-held shower. The Blue Room has a blue-velvet double canopy rope

bed so high that a step-stool is provided. There is also a trundle
bed in this room. The Brown Room, a front corner room that
faces the street, has a king-size bed and a private hall bath. The
Yellow Room, with a half-canopy double bed and fireplace, is a
lower-priced room that is a great choice if you're on a tighter
budget. When you reserve a room, be sure to indicate if you
want to sleep on a featherbed, a special feather-filled comforter.

In the dining room, the exquisite sideboard was made by
a master Amish craftsman. Pennsylvania redware plates and
handmade quilts decorate the walls. A full breakfast is served in
two seatings, usually at 8 and 9:15 A.M., and includes blueberry
waffles, blueberry pancakes, or French toast plus fresh fruit,
pastry, and juice.

Five rooms and one suite, all with private baths and fireplaces.
Weekends, rooms $95–$115; suite $170. Monday through
Thursday, rooms $65–$85; suite $140. Breakfast included.
Mannerly children and pets are welcome. Two-night stay re-
quired on weekends. No smoking. 900 West Main Street,
Ephrata, PA 17522; (717) 733-6094.

Where to Dine.   Shady Maple Smorgasbord is our favorite
of the Pennsylvania Dutch restaurants; with 1,000 seats, it's
designed for crowds. You can choose from forty-six salads,
fourteen vegetables, eight meats, eight breads, four cheeses,
three soups, ten cold desserts, three hot desserts, eight pies,
and six cakes, as well as make-your-own sundaes with every
conceivable trimming and topping. Closed Sundays. Don't come
on a holiday weekend unless you enjoy queuing up for a couple
of hours. Located on Route 23 at the intersection of Route 897.
East Earl, PA 17519; (717) 354-8222.

If you would like to dine with a Plain family and learn about
their beliefs, join River Brethren Jack Meyer, his wife, Dee
Dee, and their six children for a bounteous Pennsylvania Dutch

meal served family-style in their home. Mrs. Meyer accepts guests, including children, Monday, Tuesday, Thursday, and Saturday. Plan to arrive by 6:30 P.M. 869 Sunhill Road, Manheim, PA; (717) 664-4888.

There are two restaurants at Donecker's in Ephrata, one serving fine French cuisine and the other offering a lower-priced café menu. The creamy seafood bisque had an abundance of scallops, shrimp, and mussels and a puff-pastry lid. Healthy appetizers include grilled quail on a bed of greens, shrimp salad, or a mosaic of vegetables with a bell pepper sauce. Main courses include salmon, rack of lamb, pheasant, Dover sole, and chateaubriand. 333 North State Street, Ephrata, PA 17522; (717) 738-2421.

Windows on Steinman Park is one of our top choices for a leisurely evening of fine dining in a spectacular setting. Each of the three floors overlooks a brick courtyard dramatically illuminated in winter with tiny white lights on the branches of the honey locust trees, and in summer by floodlights shining through the leaves. An excellent Caesar salad is prepared tableside. The *fruits de mer*, puff pastry with pieces of shrimp, scallops, and lobster, is served in a cream sauce. The veal chops, stuffed with a mixture of duxelles, Gorgonzola, and spinach, sliced and served in a robust madeira sauce garnished with shiitake mushrooms, were a superb dish. Other entrées include sweetbreads, grilled venison, beef tenderloin, pheasant, and chateaubriand. 18 West King Street, Lancaster, PA 17603; (717) 295-1316. Complimentary parking is provided in the adjacent garage.

What to Do. We've visited this area many times over the years, following the Amish buggies at their fifteen-mile-per-hour gait. We've reveled in the pastoral vistas of rolling hills, immaculately kept farms, and the stark serenity of the bonneted women hanging their darkly colored quilts out to dry on the line. We've watched the men with their distinctive beards, straw hats, black trousers, and suspenders plowing as they brought order to their fields.

You could stay for weeks here and not meet an Amish person face to face. But by following the back roads, going to the markets, and stopping at their small shops, you can gain a heartfelt appreciation for a stalwart people living their own way. A detailed map of Lancaster County is a real necessity for backroad touring, visiting, and perhaps purchasing items at shops run by and catering to the Old Order Mennonites and Amish. Most of the shops are in the owners' homes, in the basement, or in an attached building or garage. There may be a small sign, or in some cases no sign at all. Never visit the stores on a Sunday, since this is truly a day of rest reserved for attending church services and visiting friends.

Stop at The People's Place on Main Street in Intercourse for an excellent introduction to the Old Order Amish and Mennonite communities. See the film and look at the hands-on collection of Amish objects and memorabilia.

Two markets worth a special trip are The Green Dragon Market on Fridays in Ephrata on Green Spot Road and Roots Market on Tuesdays in Manheim on Greystone Road. The long buildings and outdoor tables are filled chockablock with foods, clothing, and household items; crates of chickens, ducks, and rabbits are auctioned in one of the buildings; and in the early evening there is an auction with items ranging from Oriental rugs and antiques at Roots to crates of eggs and melons at The Green Dragon. Traveling through the countryside in an Amish buggy gives an appreciation for the land in a way that's not possible when you drive your car. Aaron and Jessica's Buggy Rides, located next to the Plain and Fancy Restaurant on Route 340 a few miles west of Intercourse, is owned by Jack Meyer and his daughter Jessica, who are Old Order River Brethren.

We give Martin's Pretzel Factory (1229 Diamond Street, Akron) our vote for favorite pretzels. This is a small one-room factory where you'll be able to see the entire operation and sample a pretzel as it comes out of the oven. The factory is so small that one of the girls who usually roll out the pretzels or put them in bags will stop what she is doing to help you.

If you can't get enough of antiques, plan to spend the day at Adamstown, the "Sunday Antiques Capital of the United States" (Route 272 just north of exit 21 of the Pennsylvania Turnpike), where hundreds of dealers and thousands of buyers and browsers converge in indoor and outdoor malls. Stoudt's and Renninger's are our favorites.

Other major attractions in the area include the Pennsylvania Farm Museum of Landis Valley, the Ephrata Cloister, and the Railroad Museum of Pennsylvania.

How to Get There. From the north, take the Pennsylvania Turnpike (Route 76) west to exit 21. Take Route 222 south to the Ephrata exit. Turn west on Route 322 for exactly 2.5 miles. The inn is at the corner of Main Street (Route 322) and Academy Drive.

From the south, take I-83 north to York. Take Route 30 east to Lancaster, then north on Route 222 to the Ephrata exit.

Chestnut Hill on the Delaware, *Milford, New Jersey*

Sitting in the wicker chairs on the Country Cottage's private Victorian porch overlooking the Delaware River, we couldn't help but think that this is the perfect private retreat—a place for rejuvenation or an idyllic honeymoon. The ornate nineteenth-century porch has been painstakingly stripped and painted in eight Victorian tones—shades of green, beige, a touch of cranberry, and a thin strip of gold leaf. The living room has a stereo, TV, couch, and easy chairs. A corner stove adds to the country atmosphere. Glass doors open from the living room to the bedroom, where a queen-size four-poster bed has an unobstructed view of the river. The kitchen is stocked with eggs, bread, juice, fruit, and coffee. Innkeeper Linda Castagna brings freshly baked goodies over when you arrive.

Our second favorite hideaway is next door in the main inn. The entire third floor, the bridal suite, is called Teddy's Place— a private retreat filled with one hundred and forty teddy bears at last count (many sent as presents by former guests). Once we opened a door on the second floor and climbed a steep flight of stairs, a large private space was there for us to enjoy. Teddy's Place is a two-bedroom suite: the Teddy Bear Room and Hearts and Flowers. The beds are made with crisp, lacy, white cotton designer sheets. There are monogrammed toothbrushes in the private bath. Make sure to read the room diary, replete with passages from honeymoon couples—then add your own. Teddy's Place is also a good choice for families, since there are two bedrooms. Note: Linda never rents the suite to two couples who don't know each other.

The second floor has three stunning rooms. Pineapple is a large room decorated in a yellow pattern with a private bath. The recently redecorated Bayberry Room shares a bath with Peaches and Cream. For budget-minded romantics, these shared-bath rooms are some of the nicest for the money that we've seen.

Downstairs, the informal parlor has a wood-burning fireplace. In the winter, return from a bracing walk or cross-country skiing on the old Delaware Canal towpath to mulled apple cider or hot chocolate. Curl up with a book by the fire or sit in the High Victorian Eastlake-furnished parlor with a working pump organ, a piano, and a mannequin dressed in formal Victorian attire. In warmer weather, take a cool drink out to the porch and watch the changing reflections on the river.

Breakfasts are special. Sitting in the formal dining room, we enjoyed a leisurely candlelit breakfast of freshly squeezed juice served in crystal champagne glasses, fresh fruit salad, home-made muffins, and crispy German apple pancakes. Another breakfast favorite is eggs with mushrooms, tomato, garlic, and picante sauce.

You may be interested to know that Rob, Linda's husband, has restored the inn, the Country Cottage, and two additional houses in the small town of Milford. After completing the Victorian porch, not being one to rest on his achievements, Rob has begun to create a second suite in the Country Cottage.

The Country Cottage, $130; Teddy's Place, $100 for two, $150 for four. Three additional rooms; two with shared bath, $75; one with private bath, $90. Two-night minimum on weekends. Breakfast included. Not appropriate for children. No pets. No smoking. 63 Church Street, Milford, NJ 08848; (908) 995-9761.

Where to Dine. In Milford the top choice is the Olde Mill Ford Oyster House, an unpretentious place with very reasonably priced dishes (17 Bridge Street; 908-995-9411). Try the shellfish stew, served in a large bowl brimming with mussels, clams, scallops, shrimp, and a small lobster tail. The Frenchtown Inn (Frenchtown; 908-996-3300) is a gourmet choice. We prefer to sit in the dining room with the brick walls where we have enjoyed the cabbage purses stuffed with shrimp, lobster, and crab served with two sauces, or the linguine tossed with duck sausage. If you are here on a Friday, Saturday, or Sunday night, reserve a table for an elegant, prix-fixe, seven-course dinner at EverMay on the Delaware (215-294-9100). Call ahead to see if the menu appeals, because dinner includes a choice of two entrées and two desserts. In Lambertville, New Jersey, Anton's at the Swan (43 South Main Street; 609-397-1960) changes the menu monthly. Recent appetizers include grilled scallops over pumpkin risotto or grilled sweetbreads with a wild mushroom and lentil purée, with entrées of roast pheasant with sage and pork stuffing or roast halibut with sorrel.

What to Do. The towpath along the Delaware Canal is sixty miles long and suited to hiking and bicycling. Visit New Hope, a 300-year-old artists' community. Rice's Market near New Hope is open Tuesday from 7 A.M. to noon and is a bargain hunter's delight with stalls selling everything from antiques and collectibles to sheets, clothing, furs, and wallpaper. Antiquers will want to explore the dozens of antique shops along Route 202 in Pennsylvania between New Hope and Lahaska. In the summer you can rent tubes for a leisurely float down the Delaware River or take a mule-drawn barge ride on the canal. For shoppers, there are countless high-quality outlets (Royal Doulton, Calvin Klein, Anne Klein, Harve Bernard) in Flemington, New Jersey, about twenty minutes east of Milford.

How to Get There.   From New York, take I-78 to Clinton, Route 513 south to Frenchtown, Route 29 north to Milford. From Philadelphia, take I-95 to the Route 513 south exit after Yardley on the New Jersey side of the river. Take Route 29 north to Milford.

On the verandah

The Mainstay Inn, *Cape May, New Jersey*

Sitting on the grandest Victorian veranda in Cape May, with iced tea and a plate of assorted sweets in hand, surrounded by a manicured lawn, gardens, and fountains, and listening to the horse-drawn carriages passing by the front of the inn, we couldn't imagine a better spot to soak up the Victorian era. The atmosphere of the expansive first-floor living room, with its fourteen-foot-ceiling, parlor, and dining room is impressive in its elegance. Veteran innkeepers Tom and Sue Carroll have taken this 1872 men's gambling and entertainment club and created a museum-quality environment that accurately reflects the Renaissance Revival style. While the inn is maintained to perfection, Tom and Sue definitely do not want guests to feel as though they need to tiptoe and talk in hushed tones.

The interior of the main inn is furnished with fine antiques; many are original to the house, such as the massive twelve-foot mirror in the entrance hall and the eight-foot-long brass chandelier over the dining-room table. On the ground floor are two formal parlors with floor-length windows framed by heavy swag draperies, and the dining room, where elegant breakfasts are served in the cooler months. For a view of the town, in a room only large enough for two, climb the steep stairs to the Belvedere, which is furnished with a circular couch and a ceiling painted blue with silver stars.

All of the rooms in the main inn and in the cottage next door are decorated with extreme care. Here are a few that evoke the most romantic mood. The Decatur Suite in the cottage takes up most of the third floor and has windows on four sides of the house. The sitting area is a ten-by-twelve-foot room furnished with an Eastlake parlor set and a nineteenth-century walnut writing desk. The adjoining bedroom has a carved Victorian bed that is the width of a queen-size, but is not as long. In summer, the Bret Harte Room on the second floor of the cottage is popular for its private veranda that wraps around three sides of the room, where you can spend the day lazing in the hammock or in a rocker. This bedroom, about fourteen feet square, has a massive nine-foot-tall headboard with a carving of a Shakespeare bust. The headboard towers over a queen-size bed, a matching dresser, and a rosewood parlor set. The bed is extraordinarily large; the bath, however, is one of the smaller ones at the inn.

The Cardinal's Room in the main inn is located on the second floor at the back of the house. In this corner room you'll find a double bed with an eight-foot-tall headboard and a matching nine-foot-high dresser. There is also a matched pair of armoires with wooden fronts, and a large bath. The Stonewall Jackson Suite, also in the main inn, is an extraordinarily large room with a sitting alcove, a king-size bed with a brass and iron headboard, and wicker furniture. Nine windows that wrap around three sides of the inn create a breezy feel. If you prefer a large bath, this room has the largest in the inn.

During the spring and fall, a full breakfast of a hot or cold fruit dish, an entrée such as strawberry French toast or English muffins with cheese and bacon, and homemade coffeecake is served in the formal dining room. Up to fourteen guests can sit around the dining-room table at the 8:30 or 9:30 A.M. breakfast seating. During the summer, the routine at the inn is more casual. Cereals, yogurt, fresh fruit, juices, and coffeecake are set out on the veranda for guests to help themselves. Each afternoon, tea and assorted pastries are served. As a memento you may want to add Sue's cookbook, *Breakfast at Nine, Tea at Four*, to your collection.

Note: A visit to The Mainstay, particularly during July, August, and during Victorian Week in October, must be planned well in advance. Reservations for these months are accepted beginning in January, and guests tend to ring in the New Year with a call to reserve their favorite rooms.

Open April through mid-December. Ten rooms and two suites, all with private bath; during the summer and other peak times, $135–$155; other times, $95–$145. Full breakfast included except during the summer, when there's a continental buffet. Afternoon tea included. Three-night minimum on weekends during the summer, two-night minimum on weekends at other times. One-night weekend stays, $175. Children over 12 welcome. Third person in room, $20 additional. No pets. 635 Columbia Avenue, Cape May, NJ 08204; (609) 884-8690.

Where to Dine. During the peak season there is a wide range of dining choices within walking distance of the inn. Top romantic selections include the glass-enclosed second-floor porch overlooking the beach at Maureen's (Beach Avenue and Decatur Street; 609-884-3774). Try the lobster ravioli, made with a pepper vodka cream sauce, or the creamy crab bisque. At the outdoor dining patio at 410 Bank Street (609-884-2127) we enjoyed the Cajun shellfish gumbo of lobster, sea scallops, shrimp, and smoked sausage. At Water's Edge (Beach and Pittsburgh avenues; 609-884-1717), the superb pan-fried oysters are breaded with chopped pecans and cornmeal and served with a spicy jalapeño mayonnaise. The Ebbitt Room at the Virginia Hotel (25 Jackson Street; 609-884-5700) gets better every year, especially the crabcakes and grilled tuna. The Washington Inn, a long-standing tradition in Cape May, is open year-round; favorites include the miniature crabcakes, Gorgonzola cheese tortellini, and boneless lamb chops with a minted pear and demi-glaze (801 Washington Street; 609-884-5697). The Lobster House, a huge traditional shore-dinner restaurant on Fisherman's Wharf is packed in the summer, and is one of the few places open year-round (609-884-3064). The tables along the dock are a good place to have a casual take-out meal of crabs, fried clams, shrimp, and other seafood.

What to Do. Cape May is not a one-season town. A summer vacation in Cape May could mean spending days at the beach and evenings at fine restaurants. Cape May is also an ideal place for the Victoriana buff, since it has more than 600 Victorian structures (many of them restored), gas-lit streets, and an active community committed to the preservation of this town. Take a walking tour and view the various styles of Victorian architecture

(Queen Anne, Carpenter Gothic, Mansard, Italianate, Colonial Revival, and Exotic Revival). During the spring and fall, this is one of the country's outstanding bird-watching areas. Every Thursday throughout the year the birding hotline (609-884-2626) is updated with details of sightings and information about the best places for birding.

How to Get There.   From New York City or Philadelphia, take the Garden State Parkway south to the end. Take Lafayette Street to the Washington Street Mall. Turn left on Ocean Street and left on Columbia Street.

The Queen Victoria, *Cape May, New Jersey*

Most every morning during the summer you can see innkeeper Joan Wells meticulously tending the alyssum and heather that borders this well-cared-for, distinctive 1881 corner property.

The complex includes four buildings. The newest is Prince Albert, a former rooming house that has undergone an extensive adaptive restoration and the installation of central air-conditioning. This building has six rooms and five suites. Each of the suites has its own private entrance, a pair of rocking chairs, a television, and a refrigerator. The most popular is Regents Park suite, because it is the only suite in this building with both a gas-log fireplace and a whirlpool tub. The living room has a romantic feel with dark print wallpaper and a white wicker chaise longue and chairs. The bedroom has an antique queen-size iron bed with brass trimmings and a handmade quilt; the whirlpool tub is in the handicapped-accessible bath.

There are four other suites in Prince Albert, all decorated in a similar fashion. Of these four, our preference is Hampton Court and Kew Gardens, since they have slightly larger whirlpool tubs.

On the first floor of the Carriage House, a separate building located behind the main inn, there is a sitting room with a couch, television, refrigerator, phone, as well as a bath with a whirlpool tub. The second-floor bedroom with a queen-size bed has an angled gabled ceiling.

The perfect accommodation for two couples traveling together is the Queen's Cottage, located across the street from the inn. The cottage has two rooms, each with a queen-size bed, television, and double whirlpool tub. The parlor has a gas fireplace and a pantry with a microwave oven, refrigerator, popcorn and coffee makers.

If you want to stay in the Queen Victoria building, the Prince of Wales Room has an eighteenth-century four-poster queen-size bed with a fishnet canopy. A sitting area in front of the bay windows has a partial ocean view. The Osborne Room has a gas fireplace and a double whirlpool tub. The Balmoral Room has the inn's largest double whirlpool tub. The Prince Albert Room has two double beds and a bay window seating area.

The parlor in the Queen Victoria is furnished with the clean lines of Mission style furniture, including a number of pieces made by Gustav Stickley. There is a display case of Roycroft ceramic pieces in the living room. At night and in the winter this is a jovial spot, as there is a working player piano, a fireplace, a decanter of sherry, and a popcorn popper. There's a second common room in Prince Albert.

Thoughtful touches include twice-daily maid service, a specially made chocolate on your pillow at night, a basket of toiletries, a choice of foam or feather pillows, bicycles to borrow, and extra towels to use at the beach.

Guests can choose to have their breakfast in the dining room at the Queen Victoria, the Prince Albert, or have it brought to their room anytime from 8 to 10 A.M. Joan and her husband Dane host the full breakfast of granola and other cereals, fresh fruit, an egg dish, juice, muffins, breads, and Wolferman's English muffins, all served buffet style.

Joan, a former director of the Victorian Society in Philadelphia, has a wealth of knowledge about the Victorian period. Guests who visit on the first weekend after Thanksgiving weekend can help decorate the inn's authentic Victorian Christmas trees. At Christmas and Thanksgiving, Joan said, "We become an extended family as we plan special weekends to include our guests."

Twenty-three rooms, suites, and cottages, all with private bath. Mid-June through mid-September, $120–$160, suites, $175–$205. Midweek rates during the summer are $5 to $25 less per room. Lower rates at other times of the year. Full breakfast and afternoon refreshments included. Minimum stay of three to four nights during the season and two nights on weekends the rest of the year. Children welcome; third person in room, $20 additional. No pets. 102 Ocean Street, Cape May, NJ 08204; (609) 884-8702.

Where to Dine. During the peak season there is a wide range of dining choices within walking distance of the inn. Top romantic choices include the glass-enclosed second-floor porch overlooking the beach at Maureen's (Beach Avenue and Decatur Street; 609-884-3774). Try the lobster ravioli, made with a pepper vodka cream sauce, or the creamy crab bisque.

At the outdoor dining patio at 410 Bank Street (609-884-2127) we enjoyed the Cajun shellfish gumbo of lobster, sea scallops, shrimp, and smoked sausage. At Water's Edge (Beach and Pittsburgh avenues; 609-884-1717), the superb pan-fried oysters are breaded with chopped pecans and cornmeal and served with a spicy jalapeño mayonnaise.

The Ebbitt Room at the Virginia Hotel (25 Jackson Street; 609-884-5700) gets better every year; crabcakes and grilled tuna are specialties. The Washington Inn, a long-standing tradition in Cape May, is open year-round; favorite dishes include the miniature crabcake, the Gorgonzola cheese tortellini, and the boneless lamb chops with a minted pear and demi-glaze (801 Washingon Street; 609-884-5697). The Lobster House, a huge traditional shore-dinner restaurant on Fisherman's Wharf, is packed in the summer, and is one of the few places open year-round (609-884-3064). The tables along the dock are a good place to have a casual take-out meal of crabs, fried clams, shrimp, and other seafood.

What to Do.   Cape May is not a one-season town. A summer vacation in Cape May could mean spending days at the beach and evenings at fine restaurants. Cape May is also an ideal place for the Victoriana buff, since it has more than 600 Victorian structures (many of them restored), gas-lit streets, and an active community committed to the preservation of this town. Take a walking tour and view the various styles of Victorian architecture (Queen Anne, Carpenter Gothic, Mansard, Italianate, Colonial Revival, and Exotic Revival). During the spring and fall, this is one of the country's outstanding bird-watching areas. Every Thursday throughout the year the birding hotline (609-884-2626) is updated with details of sightings and information about the best places for birding.

How to Get There. From New York or Philadelphia take the Garden State Parkway to the end. Continue on Lafayette Street south to the Washington Street Mall. Turn left on Ocean Street to the inn.

JANE STAUFFER

Brampton, *Chestertown, Maryland*

In the heart of Maryland's Eastern Shore, two miles from the center of Chestertown on fifteen acres of woodland and farmland, stands this 1860 Greek Revival manor house, which is listed on the National Register of Historic Places. Owners Danielle and Michael Hanscom have the qualities that spell success in the innkeeping profession: the cordial hospitality Danielle perfected in her former job as a Swissair flight attendant, and the ingenuity and restoration skills Michael honed on renovating Victorian homes in San Francisco. Sharing the dream of working together, the Hanscoms have combined good taste and lots of hard work to create a picturesque hideaway.

With its twelve-foot ceilings, the living room has an airy, uncluttered feeling. When we commented on the difficulty of getting books down from the bookcases that reached to the ceiling, Danielle pointed to the top shelf where she had stashed a collection of calculus books and said, "I really don't have much need for them." The focal point of the room is the pair of matching sensuous gray glove-leather couches that Danielle brought from Switzerland. These face each other on an Oriental rug next to a fireplace. On the other side of the room there is an ornate Victorian couch.

The solid walnut staircase leads up to two large second-floor bedrooms with eleven-foot ceilings, and a suite. The most romantic room in the house is the Yellow Room with a curly maple, queen-size, lacy canopy bed, down comforter, European armoire, easy chairs, and a working fireplace. We liked the romance of lying in bed under the down duvet and watching the soft glow of the embers. Equally attractive is the Blue Room on the second floor, which has twin beds with white duvet covers. These can be made into a king-size bed if requested. The placement of the two easy chairs is ideal for reading by the working fireplace. A second-floor suite with a lower ceiling includes a four-poster pencil-post double bed as well as a twin bed and a television, but no fireplace. This is the only room that has a television.

The third-floor Red and Green rooms are the same size as the second-floor rooms, but have nine-foot ceilings and wood-burning Franklin stoves instead of fireplaces. Each room has a desk and two reading chairs. The furnishings reflect the Swiss penchant for uncluttered sophistication. The Green Room is a bit more romantic, as there is a lacy canopy over the queen-size bed and a large armoire with a mirrored door. The Rose Room, which has a king-size bed and a sitting area, is accessible by a private staircase (a problem if you're tall, as you need to duck as you go up the stairs).

A plate of fresh fruit is in each room. Danielle also offers refreshments in the afternoon and sherry or wine after dinner. We enjoyed the thin, crisp buttery cookies.

The large first-floor breakfast room is furnished with Swiss antiques crafted in the late nineteenth century. Breakfast includes freshly squeezed orange juice, fruit, muffins or coffeecake, a choice of eggs, sausage, French toast, or possibly a Swiss specialty such as bread and butter pudding with strawberry sauce.

Danielle and Michael live on the property with their two children in a (much) converted animal hospital. Also on the premises are two friendly dogs: a chocolate-colored Labrador and a white mixed-breed. There's plenty of room for the dogs and guests to roam.

Five rooms and one suite, all with private baths, $90–$120. Full breakfast included. Children permitted with prior arrangements. Third person in room, $25 additional. No pets. One mile south of Chestertown on Route 20. 25227 Chestertown Road, Chestertown, MD 21620; (410) 778-1860.

Where to Dine.   The Imperial Hotel in Chestertown (208 High Street; 410-778-5000) features regional American cuisine. Appetizers include grilled oysters served with country bacon, a medley of wild mushrooms served with roasted garlic, grilled duck sausage, and clam bisque with sweet corn. The sautéed filet of rock fish is served with stewed leeks, chives and oyster cream. Pan-seared salmon comes with roasted corn, lime, and cilantro.

The casual, moderately priced Ironstone Café is a favorite (236 Cannon Street; 410-778-0188). We enjoyed the large individually tossed salad of red and green leaf lettuce with a garlic-mustard vinaigrette, and plump, tender oysters baked and presented on a bed of spinach topped with minced Smithfield ham and cream sauce.

If you enjoy spicy hard-shell crabs, you can spend a couple of glorious hours by the water enjoying the view and picking the crabs at Waterman's Crab House (Sharp Street Wharf, Rock Hall; 410-639-2261).

What to Do. Stroll around Chestertown, especially along the streets by the river, where you'll see fine eighteenth-century homes in this former Colonial trading port. Stop by the chamber of commerce for a walking-tour map. At the north end of town is Washington College, a small liberal arts school to which George Washington donated money and his name. You may also want to visit Oxford and St. Michaels, about an hour's drive south. The area is very flat and there are plenty of back roads for bicycling. If you have an interest in auctions, visit Dixon's Auctions in Crumpton. Held every Wednesday throughout the year, this is one of the largest auctions on the East Coast, spread out over six large fields and a large building.

How to Get There. From Washington, D.C., take the Bay Bridge, then take Route 301 north to Route 213. From Philadelphia, take I-95 south. Exit at Route 279, then take Route 213 to Chestertown.

JANE STAUFFER

The Inn at Perry Cabin, *St. Michaels, Maryland*

Sitting in the Morning Room on a cold January afternoon, we watched and listened as a flock of several hundred honking Canadian geese landed in Fogg Cove. A formally attired waiter set in front of us a large wooden tray that held a pot of tea and an extra pot of hot water along with lemon slices, cream, sugar, and little plates filled with scones, dishes of whipped cream and raspberry jam, banana and nut breads, and assorted cookies. We were totally relaxed and felt properly pampered.

The inn, owned by Sir Bernard Ashley, co-founder of the Laura Ashley retail empire, was created according to his vision of an English country house hotel. More than $6 million was spent in expanding and refurbishing the original Colonial Revival waterfront mansion and the surrounding twenty-five acres bordering the Miles River.

The atmosphere at The Inn at Perry Cabin is one of hushed, sophisticated elegance. On the first floor there are three sitting rooms overlooking the water, one with a fireplace. Sofas and chairs, upholstered in Ashley fabrics, are grouped for ease of conversation; thick carpeting is overlaid with Oriental rugs; shelves are filled with English china; quantities of antique and reproduction furniture and small collectibles give the inn a home-like feel. There are picture books and magazines, baskets of fruit and nuts, fresh and dried flower arrangements, shelves of old English titles, and tables and mantles where decorative tin boxes, glass paperweights, walking canes with ivory handles, old bottles, bowls of potpourri, and old photographs are artfully placed.

Each of the bedrooms is decorated with different coordinated Ashley fabrics. It's a designer's showcase, combining the bright or subtle patterns of the polished cottons with antiques or repro-duction antiques. Most of the rooms have queen-size beds. In each room you'll find fresh flowers, mineral water, a plate of fruit, a remote-controlled color television, telephone, and indi-vidually controlled heating and air-conditioning. Baths have ter-rycloth robes, hair dryers, English toiletries, thick towels, and most have heated towel racks. We had a hard time getting used to the English-style sink with separate hot and cold water faucets.

The newest section of the inn has twenty-one rooms and suites, all with water views. There are four duplex suites. Two have a bedroom on the upper level and two have an upper-level sitting room. Three of the suites in this section have Jacuzzi tubs. Many of the rooms have doors that open onto a small terrace or patio. A common room is set for playing snooker (a game similar to billiards).

The best room in the other part of the inn is the bridal suite, which has a private balcony off the bedroom overlooking the water and a separate sitting room. The deluxe queen-studio suite, underneath the bridal suite, has a doorway leading to a brick terrace and to one of the public sitting rooms. Other rooms have terraces or balconies with views of Fogg Cove or the front of the inn.

There are six rooms in the older original section, furnished with antiques. A number of these rooms and suites have front views overlooking the river, but the windows are smaller than in the newer section; the rooms are darker, and you need to go to the window to appreciate the view.

Facilities at the inn include a fitness center, steam shower, pool with optional current to swim against, and bicycles for exploring the area. Afternoon tea is served from 3 to 5 P.M.

Guests can choose anything they want from the extensive breakfast menu. Choices include fresh juices, berries, and melon; among main entrées are thin buttermilk pancakes filled with chopped fresh fruit, cinnamon, lemon, and brown sugar; Belgian pecan waffles with maple syrup; eggs Benedict with smoked salmon, country ham, or black truffles; a crab and potato omelet; or Welsh rarebit.

When you come to dinner you are treated as a house guest. You may have a cocktail in one of the three parlors before being seated at your table. The main dining room, the Ashley Room, has a two-story peaked ceiling from which hang a pair of elaborate crystal chandeliers. Nine widely spaced candlelit tables, a large wood-burning fireplace, Ashley-print wallpaper and table-cloths, crimson upholstered chairs, marble busts, an old English buffet, and a wall of windows overlooking the water make this a beautiful setting.

At a five-course winter dinner we started with tartare of oysters and seared foie gras served with glazed apples and a rich port sauce. The mussel soup had a hint of orange and saffron flavor, and a salad of baby greens with chopped duck confit had a hazelnut and truffle oil dressing. Entrées included loin of lamb with sweetbreads, lemon sole and shrimp, gratin of lobster and oysters, medallions of salmon, and grilled breast of duck.

The most popular dessert is a combination plate of dense chocolate pâté, a bittersweet chocolate marquise, and a scoop of white chocolate ice cream. Other choices are chocolate mille-feuille, lemon torte served with lemon ice cream, apple dowdy, pear tart, or shortbread with raspberry coulis.

Thirty-five rooms and six suites. Rooms, $205–$325; suites, $375–$500. Lunch daily, 12 to 2:30 P.M., $14.95–$25. Dinner 6 to 9:30 P.M.; prix-fixe dinner, $50. Full breakfast and afternoon tea included. Children over 10 welcome. No pets. 308 Watkins Lane, St. Michaels, MD 21663; (800) 722-2949 or (410) 745-2200.

What to Do. Don't miss the Chesapeake Bay Maritime Museum, where visitors can trace the history of the Chesapeake Bay and its early inhabitants from the Ice Age to the present day. Informative displays explain the trading of tobacco with England, the harvesting of crabs and oysters, and waterfowl hunting with flocks of wooden decoys and guns. At dockside, look at the floating fleet: a skipjack, a Virginia crab dredger, and a buy boat. Take a cruise on the Patriot, and gorge on hard-shell crabs at the Crab Claw restaurant (Navy Point; 410-745-2900).

From St. Michaels, drive twelve winding miles west on Route 33 past fields of corn to Knapps Narrows drawbridge, one of the busiest in the East, and the Bay Hundred Restaurant (Route 33 and Knapps Narrows, Tilghman; 410-886-2622). If you are here in the early afternoon, you can see the watermen returning with their catch. After crossing the bridge to Tilghman Island, the road continues for three miles past a skipjack harbor where you can see the last remaining working fishing sailboats in the United States. Continue on to Harrison's Chesapeake House, where you might wish to arrange for a day of fishing on the bay (Route 33; 410-886-2123).

Drive over to Oxford, taking the tiny ferry from Bellevue, and have lunch at the Robert Morris Inn. Note the numerous boatyards and well-maintained homes. Drive down Pier Street past the Pier Street Marina to the U.S. Bureau of Commercial Fisheries Biological Laboratory. If you are there during business hours, ask for a tour and learn about research on the decline of the oyster catch.

How to Get There. From Philadelphia, go south on I-95 to Route 896 south. At the end of Route 896, go south on Route 301. Turn left (south) on Route 213 to Route 50. Go east on Route 50 to Easton. Go west on Route 33 to St. Michaels.

From Washington, D.C., take Route 50 east over the Chesapeake Bay Bridge, then follow the above directions.

Porch of Sandaway Lodge at Robert Morris Inn

Robert Morris Inn, *Oxford, Maryland*

Located along the banks of the Tred Avon River on Maryland's Eastern Shore, Oxford is a sleepy little town that has worked to maintain the mood of a bygone era, when time was measured by the coming and going of sailing ships. Here you'll find no fast-food restaurants, no supermarkets, and no shopping centers.

But a couple looking for a shaded porch, spectacular sunsets over the water, a friendly community, and traditional Eastern Shore seafood may find the Robert Morris Inn to be the perfect place. Long-time innkeepers Wendy and Ken Gibson have preserved the charm of the old inn and also have added new buildings along the water for guests who prefer a more modern ambience.

Built prior to 1710, when Oxford was a major port in the region, the main inn was named after the father of one of the major financiers of the American Revolution, who lived here from 1738 to 1750. Fortunately, much of the original inn survives today. If you want to absorb the Colonial flavor, reserve a room in the original section, complete with creaky, slightly slanting floors and handmade wall paneling. You'll appreciate the Elizabethan-style enclosed staircase, the Georgia white-pine flooring in the upstairs hall, and fireplaces made of English bricks brought to Oxford as ballast in trading ships. On the second floor are two of the original rooms that date back to 1710. Room 1 has a double bed and room 2 has a double bed with a canopy; both have side views of the river. The other two original rooms are on the third floor, room 15 with a double canopy bed and room 17 with a double bed; these also have side views of the river. On the third floor of the main inn are three rooms with king-size beds: rooms 19, 20, and 25.

We prefer to stay in the Victorian Sandaway Lodge, about a block from the main inn, or the recently constructed River Rooms that overlook the Tred Avon River. Here, in a quiet, tranquil setting, you can laze away the day sitting on your private porch or on a blanket at the water's edge.

At Sandaway, each room is designed with slight variations. Rooms 101 and 102 are riverfront rooms with queen-size beds; room 201 has two twin beds; and room 202 has a king-size four-poster. Each room has a private balcony perfect for warm-weather relaxing. Room 301 on the third floor is a riverfront room with a sitting room, large bathroom with both a tub and a shower, and a king-size pencil-post bed. Room 105 has a large bathroom with gold Sherle Wagner fixtures, a king-size lace canopy bed that was once in Washington, D.C., at the Blair House; and a side view of the river. Room 103 was made into a wheelchair-accessible room.

Next door are the popular and particularly romantic River Rooms. Each has a private, screened-in porch, a picture window overlooking the water, a spacious bathroom with both a clawfoot tub and a shower, and a king-size four-poster bed. Rooms 107 and 109 are on the first floor; rooms 108 and 110 are on the second floor.

For meals, the pumpkin-colored main inn is a pleasant stroll away. At breakfast and lunch we were seated in the comfortably casual tavern room with a slate floor, dark wood-paneled walls, and open wood-burning fireplace. Adjoining the tavern room is the formal dining room. Of note are the impressive murals made from 140-year-old wallpaper samples. The original wallpaper of this design is in the reception room of the White House.

The menu has remained basically the same over the twenty years in which we have frequented the Eastern Shore. The Robert Morris has made its reputation by serving honest food cooked by chefs without pedigrees. The menu is straightforward, with dishes such as fried shrimp, scallops, or crabcakes, broiled seafood imperial, stuffed shrimp, filet of fish, and prime rib. The inn is famous for its crab dishes. Maryland blue-crab aficionados will be interested to know that the crab is usually at its best in September and October.

Thirty-five rooms with private bath, $80–$200. One two-bedroom apartment suitable for a family. Breakfast available but not included in the room rate. Children over 10 welcome. All rooms are equipped for double occupancy only (except the apartment). No pets. April through November, breakfast, 8 to 11 A.M.; lunch, 1 to 3 P.M., $2.95–$17.95; dinner 6 to 9 P.M., entrées, $10.95–$27.95. The dining room is closed on Tuesday.

December through March, restaurant hours vary. 312 Morris
Street, Oxford, MD 21654; (410) 226–5111.

How to Get There.   From Philadelphia, go south on I-95
to Route 896 south. At the end of Route 896, go south on Route
301. Turn left (south) on Route 213 to Route 50. Go east on
Route 50 through Easton. Go west on Route 33 to Oxford.

From Washington, D.C., take Route 50 east over the Chesapeake Bay Bridge, then follow the above directions.

What to Do.   Start a fifty-mile excursion at the Robert
Morris Inn in Oxford. Drive along The Strand, then down Mill
Street past The Masthead. Note the numerous boatyards and
well-maintained homes. Down Pier Street past the Pier Street
Marina is a U.S. Bureau of Commercial Fisheries Biological
Laboratory, where research is done on the decline of the oyster
catch. If you are here during business hours, ask for a tour.
After you've seen Oxford, cross the Tred Avon River on the
little auto ferry. The ferry lands in Bellevue. Follow the road for
about four miles to Royal Oak, then bear left on Route 33 into
St. Michaels. According to local legend, during the War of 1812
St. Michaels' townspeople put lanterns high in the trees and
extinguished all other lights, making an approaching British fleet
think that the town was on a bluff. Consequently, the British
cannon fire overshot the town and St. Michaels was saved. In
St. Michaels, take the road to Navy Point. Visit the Chesapeake
Bay Maritime Museum, gorge on crabs at the Crab Claw, take
a cruise on the Patriot, and explore the harbor area.

From St. Michaels, Route 33 winds past fields of corn.
Twelve miles from St. Michaels, you arrive at Knapps Narrows
drawbridge, one of the busiest in the eastern United States,
and the Bay Hundred Restaurant. If you are here in the early
afternoon, you can see the watermen returning with their catch.
After crossing the bridge to Tilghman Island, the road continues

for three miles past a skipjack harbor where you can see the last remaining working fishing sailboats in the United States. Continue on to Harrison's Chesapeake House, where you may wish to arrange for a day of fishing on the bay.

Mr. Mole is the corner row house on far right.

Mr. Mole Bed and Breakfast, *Baltimore, Maryland*

This spacious Bolton Hill brick row house, named after that wonderful character in Kenneth Grahame's *Wind in the Willows* who is always spring cleaning, was totally renovated by innkeepers Paul Bragaw and Collin Clarke with private baths, central air-conditioning, a fire alarm and sprinkler system, and telephones in each room. It is decorated like a designer's showcase home, the kind we'd gladly pay to have the opportunity just to tour. Each floor of the 1870s house has a different color and theme. The first floor has fourteen-foot ceilings, two crystal chandeliers, bright yellow walls, and blue and yellow madras draperies and upholstery. There are nonworking marble fireplaces, display cases with ecclesiastical antiques and manuscripts, a collection of early nineteenth-century snuff boxes, blue and white Oriental pots tucked everywhere, and a Baldwin concert grand piano that's kept in tune.

We stayed in The Print Room on the second floor, which has a gray leather couch and chair facing a carved nonworking Italian marble fireplace and an elegant gilded cornice over the queen-size bed. A second smaller bedroom in this suite has an antique quilt hung over the double bed and child-size pieces of twig furniture mounted on the wall. There are fresh flowers in all the rooms, color-coordinated to the decor.

The London Suite on the third floor has a dramatic red queen-size bed with a red and white checkered canopy with a green lining that matches the comforter, window treatment, and upholstery.

The Garden Room is bright and more informal than the other rooms with hanging dried flowers, emerald green wall-to-wall carpet, and a queen-size bed with a padded flowered headboard to match the painting on the wall. French doors open onto a plant-filled sunroom with white wicker furniture.

Mr. Mole's House, a lower-level wheelchair-accessible room with its own side entrance, has a queen-size canopy bed, two easy chairs, and a collection of early nineteenth-century English teapots. We spied a picture of Mr. Mole, Ratty, Badger, and Toad, whom we imagined were hatching some devious plot, on spool shelves above the desk.

Breakfast is served buffet style (seatings at 8 and 9 A.M.), and guests sit at individual tables. When we remarked that the brown-sugar cream cheese pie and the apple walnut crumb cake looked very rich, Paul told us, "I live with the philosophy that life is too short not to have dessert first." We also sampled loaves of homemade whole-wheat and rum ginger raisin breads, a platter of sliced cheeses and meats, and a bowl of fresh fruit.

Other nice touches are the glass of sherry and the little box of chocolates that were in our room, as well as afternoon tea with cakes and cucumber sandwiches that the innkeepers will prepare with advance notice.

Five rooms and suites, all with private bath, $85–$115. A second bedroom, which accommodates one person, is available in two of the suites for $25 additional. Breakfast (and tea, if requested) is included. Children over 10 welcome, $25 additional. Parking garage on the premises. No smoking. No pets. 1601 Bolton Street, Baltimore, MD 21217; (410) 728-1179.

Where to Dine.   For elegant dining, our choice is Hampton's in the Harbor Court Hotel (550 Light Street; 410-234-0550). Call ahead and reserve one of the four coveted window tables with fabulous views overlooking the activity of the Inner Harbor. For starters there's venison sausage ragout and grilled shiitake mushrooms piled high with a mixture of lobster, crab, and shrimp. Continue with slices of rare loin of lamb accompanied by a white bean and slivered sun-dried tomato garnish, and seared scallops with black bean crêpes. For dessert try the sampler, a smaller portion of the five desserts that are on the evening's menu.

In the Fell's Point section of Baltimore our favorite is Pierpoint (1822 Aliceanna; 410-675-2080). This narrow eighteen-table storefront open-kitchen bistro restaurant features such dishes as smoked silver queen corn chowder, cioppino made with a rich crab stock, and crabcakes made with smoked crab meat. Foster's Oyster Bar (606 South Broadway; 410-558-3600), also in Fell's Point, is where we go to sit at the bar and have a dozen raw Chincoteague oysters and a beer.

Tio Pepe (10 East Franklin Street; 410-539-4675), now in its twenty-fifth year, features Castilian Spanish dishes such as the Zarzuela de Mariscos Costa Brava, a shellfish stew brought sizzling to the table; Valenciana paella, made with chicken, chorizo sausage, shrimp, clams, mussels, and saffron rice; or our favorite, roast suckling pig (we suggest you call ahead to reserve a portion). Louie's Bookstore Café (518 North Charles Street; 410-962-1224) is the place where the young fine-arts crowd hangs out. A bookstore is in front and there's a two-level restaurant in the back, featuring performances by young musicians from the Peabody Conservatory of Music, which is across the street, and dishes such as omelets, stir-fries, and hijiki and tofu, a Japanese noodle-like seaweed sautéed with vegetables served over brown rice. If you like crabcakes, stop at Faidley's Seafood in the sprawling Lexington Market for the best crabcakes in Baltimore.

What to Do.   Through brilliant planning, beginning in the 1960s, the center of Baltimore has been rebuilt and the Inner Harbor's rotting piers turned into a magnificent public promenade. Harborplace, two glass buildings filled with interesting shops and restaurants, opened in July 1980. This was the beginning of Baltimore's renaissance. The city that once was known as "the armpit of the East" turned into the Cinderella city of the United States. The National Aquarium, the crown jewel of the Inner Harbor, opened in August 1981. Its success has dwarfed all expectations, with crowds lining up daily. Hotels and office buildings were built and the old houses in the nearby neighborhoods of Otterbein, Federal Hill, and Fell's Point were rehabilitated. "Plaaaaaaay ball!" was heard on April 6, 1992, at the brand new $105 million, 48,000-seat, old-fashioned baseball park, the new home for the Baltimore Orioles, just four blocks from the Inner Harbor. Fell's Point, an area of the city along the waterfront, is slowly being gentrified with a number of restaurants and bars that attract a college-age crowd on the weekends. A water taxi runs from Fell's Point to the Inner Harbor.

Railroad fans will want to visit the B&O Railroad Museum, housed in a 123-foot tall, 22-sided roundhouse built in 1884. The Walters Art Gallery has 25,000 objects housed in three connected buildings: an 1850 Italianate town mansion, a Renaissance palace built in 1904, and a contemporary gallery built in 1974. The superb collection of Chinese and Japanese porcelains and Japanese lacquers and metalwork is displayed in the mansion just as a wealthy nineteenth-century patron of the arts would have shown his collection. The Baltimore Museum of Art has the outstanding Cone collection of modern art, including paintings from every year of Matisse's work between 1917 and 1940. There are numerous early works by Picasso, and paintings by van Gogh, Gauguin, and Cézanne.

How to Get There. From the north, take I-95 south to the Baltimore Beltway (I-695) toward Towson. Take I-83 south to exit 6 (North Avenue/Mt. Royal Avenue). Go south one block on Mt. Royal Avenue. Turn right at the light on McMechen Street. Go two blocks to the stop sign at Bolton Street.

From the south, take I-95 north. Take exit 53 to I-395 as you approach the city. Go .8 mile and bear right on Martin Luther King, Jr., Boulevard. Go two miles and turn left on Eutaw Street. Turn right (at the fourth light) onto McMechen Street. Bolton Street is the next intersection.

JANE STAUFFER

Ashby Inn, *Paris, Virginia*

We sat on our private deck sipping coffee and looking out to the pastoral foothills of the Blue Ridge Mountains in the village of Paris, Virginia (population 60). A herd of cattle and groups of deer were browsing on the hillside. We couldn't help but be thoroughly impressed with the creative way that innkeepers John and Roma Sherman have converted the village's original one-room schoolhouse, located two doors down the street from the main inn, into four spacious, airy rooms.

For a romantic getaway, these rooms are our top picks. The two rooms on the top floor (our preference) have cathedral ceilings. Each of these rooms has a pencil-post queen-size canopy bed that faces the wall of windows and a glass door that leads to a private balcony. Other features include a wood-burning fireplace, two easy chairs, a long window seat, and a large bath with a deep soaking tub. Rooms are color-coordinated, from the balloon curtains to the upholstery on the window seat and wingback chairs. These four rooms also have coffee makers (a great feature for those who love to have a cup of coffee in bed or on the balcony) as well as televisions and telephones. After a day spent touring the back roads and visiting the vineyards, it is delightful to sit in front of your own fireplace or on a private balcony overlooking the scenic hillside. Look closely and you may spot fox hunters or hikers on the Appalachian Trail, which passes along the top of the ridge.

In the main inn there are six rooms, a fine restaurant, and an English pub. Before the new rooms were constructed our favorite was the large Fan Room, a quiet room with a balcony that overlooks the hillside. This room has a Palladian window that matches the shape of the headboard on the queen-size bed. The Fireplace Room is the only one in the main inn with its own wood-burning fireplace. All the rooms are furnished with antiques and country furniture that the Shermans have collected throughout the Shenandoah Valley. Oriental and rag rugs soften polished wood floors, and hunt prints evoke Roma's passion for the sport.

In the warm weather our hearty country breakfast of muffins, eggs any style, potatoes, bacon and sausage, juice, and coffee was served outside on the patio. The scent of fresh hay in adjacent fields prompted us to contemplate settling in this idyllic Jeffersonian village.

The inn is located in the midst of horse country, so conversation often centers on the activities of the horsy set. Roma rides regularly and welcomes any questions about the sport or where to see a hunt. John, who has done a lot of political speechwriting, can fill many hours with fascinating tales.

We like the casual feeling of the dining rooms. The pub room, with a working fireplace, is cozy on a winter night. The porch room has big windows, and another room has high-backed private booths for intimate conversation.

Appetizers on a recent winter menu include steamed mussels, gravlax, pheasant and pistachio sausage, grilled shrimp with Szechuan eggplant salad, and fried calamari. From a previous summer visit we remember the crabcakes made with jumbo lump crabmeat fresh from Maryland's Eastern Shore. Winter entrées included grilled monkfish with shiitake mushroom risotto, roast leg of lamb with creamed spinach and rosemary potatoes, winter seafood stew with rouille and garlic bread, and Parmesan-crusted swordfish.

The Sunday buffet brunch is a favorite of the locals, many of whom dine here so regularly that they call only when they're not coming. On a recent Sunday in December we started with a hearty peasant soup filled with sausage and potatoes. The brunch line started with omelets made to order by Roma and continued with a whole ham that John carved and piled on buttermilk biscuits. Other selections included chicken curry, wild rice and tenderloin salad, and a seafood stew covered with crispy phyllo crust. Dessert was a deep-dish apple crisp accompanied by thick whipped cream.

Ten rooms, eight with private bath, $80–$175; $15–$20 additional charge for Saturday night stay only. Full breakfast included. Children over 10 welcome; $20 additional for third person in room. No pets. Dinner served Wednesday through Saturday, 6 to 9 P.M. Entrées, $13.25–$19.50. Sunday brunch, 12 to 2:30 P.M., $20.95. Paris, VA 22130; (703) 592-3900.

What to Do. Take a drive through the 195,000-acre Shenandoah National Park, which has hiking trails, nature walks, waterfalls and some of the finest vistas in the East. Watch the start of a fox hunt. Go to the point-to-point or steeplechase races which are held on spring and fall weekends. Tour the large plantation homes such as Oatlands or Morven Park. Visit the impressive stalagmite and stalactite formations at Luray Caverns. Wine lovers will find much to appreciate in the growing number of Virginia vineyards: Naked Mountain Vineyards in Markham, Linden Vineyards in Linden, and Oasis Vineyard in Hume are a few favorites. Visit a shiitake mushroom farm in

Amissville or the Holy Cross Abbey in Berryville, home of Trappist monks who bake and supply bread to area supermarkets. Go antiquing or simply stroll the sidewalks of a secluded historic village like Waterford, Virginia.

How to Get There. Paris is 60 miles west of Washington, D.C., at the intersection of Routes 17 and 50. From Washington, take Route 50 west through Middleburg. Three miles west of Upperville, turn left on Route 759 (300 yards beyond the traffic light). From the Beltway (I-495), take Route 66 west to exit 5 (Delaplane/Paris), continue 7.5 miles north on Route 17, then left on Route 701, which runs into the village.

The Inn at Little Washington,
Washington, Virginia

What causes a couple to willingly pay an extra $80 to $120 to dine and lodge on a Friday or Saturday night in a tiny Virginia town? What is so extraordinary to cause the flurry of articles, the five-star Mobil award, the AAA Five Diamond Award, and designation as the only "Relais Gourmand" hotel in the United States? What is the reason that a stream of limousines, even the occasional helicopter, brings well-heeled patrons to The Inn at Little Washington?

We think it's the very real possibility that the inn will fulfill your romantic dreams of being pampered in a grand Victorian English country home.

If you are going to invest in this experience, we suggest you choose one of the two duplex suites located on the third and fourth floors of the inn. The favorite is room 9, which overlooks the landscaped inner garden courtyard; the other duplex overlooks the street and Blue Ridge mountains beyond. You'll walk from your sitting room, which includes a balcony, to the second floor of the duplex, a luxuriously appointed bedroom with another balcony.

The superior rooms have king-size beds and a balcony. The best is room 5, which is directly over the center of the garden courtyard. Rooms 3 and 7 also have a view of the garden. The intermediate rooms are slightly smaller and have a queen-size bed and a bay window with a window seat. There is only one standard room, which has a queen-size bed and a bath with a shower only.

We didn't want to leave. The rooms included English antiques, canopy beds, faux bois woodwork, flowers in profusion, mints, fruit, expensive coffee-table books, a stocked minibar. The luxurious marble baths included a Jacuzzi, heated towel racks, thick terrycloth robes, hair-dryers, and fine soaps.

Across the street there is a guest house with two accommodations, one of which is a two-bedroom suite with a living room; French doors open onto a balcony and a full kitchen. This would be a good choice for a family or for entertaining guests.

Breakfast is served in the glass-enclosed pavilion that faces the courtyard. Included with the room is freshly squeezed orange juice, fresh fruits served with crème fraîche, croissants, and Danish. A hot entrée such as French toast, corned-beef hash, or grilled trout is available for an additional charge. Owners Patrick O'Connell and Reinhardt Lynch have recently purchased the local post office, which they are converting to a café with an outdoor dining terrace.

During the day, the large staff quietly cleans, polishes, arranges flowers, and somehow manages to keep the whole place in a state of perfection.

With that kind of introduction, you shouldn't be surprised to learn that dinner here is simply superb. You can start with carpaccio of baby lamb, foie gras sautéed with ham, chilled grilled figs with ham, or lobster napoleon with caviar. The between-course selections include sorbet or salad. Choosing among the ten main courses can be difficult. Entrées might include filet of beef served on a tangle of tart greens; grilled lobster with orzo; peppered tuna and swordfish grilled rare; or three veal medallions each served a different way—with a purée of black olives, with sun-dried tomatoes and pesto, and in a minestrone broth. No matter which extraordinary entrée you choose, you'll find it beautifully prepared and presented.

The desserts are equally extravagant. In early spring the rhubarb mousse is special, but we also recommend the unusual grapefruit pecan chocolate tart.

Ten rooms. Standard room, $230; intermediate rooms, $280; superior rooms, $340. Two duplex suites, $460 each. Guest house, $250, $390. Friday, Saturday, holidays, and the month of October, $80 surcharge per room. Weekends are booked two to three months in advance. Continental breakfast included; additional charge for full breakfast. Overnight guests have guaranteed dinner reservations at the restaurant, which opens for dinner Monday and Wednesday through Friday, 6 to 9:30 P.M.; Saturday, 5:30 to 9:30 P.M.; Sunday, 4 to 9:30 P.M. Prix fixe for appetizer, entrée, sorbet or salad, dessert, and coffee, $78 per person ($88 on Saturday night). Middle and Main Streets, Washington, VA 22747; (703) 675-3800.

What to Do. Stroll around the village and visit the high-quality craft, art, antique, and custom-furniture galleries. Taste Virginia wines at local vineyards. The following are nearby and have regular tasting hours: Naked Mountain Vineyards in Markham, Linden vineyards in Linden, and Oasis Vineyard in Hume. Visit the 195,000-acre Shenandoah National Park with hiking trails, nature walks, waterfalls, and some of the finest scenic vistas in the East. Trail rides are available at the Marriott Ranch; call (703) 364-2627 for reservations. Or, follow the back roads in Middleburg and Fauquier counties to see the panoramas enjoyed by the fox hunters.

How to Get There. From Washington, D.C., take the Beltway (I-495) to I-66 west to exit 10-A Gainesville. Follow Route 29 south to Warrenton. In Warrenton, take Route 211 west. Turn right on 211 Business to Washington, Virginia.

JANE STAUFFER

Conyers House, *Sperryville, Virginia*

This rambling country inn, owned and operated by Sandra and Norman Cartwright-Brown, is situated on a country road in the midst of the Virginia hunt country, an area that borders the Shenandoah Mountains.

Sandra, an avid fox hunter, keeps her thoroughbred hunting horse and a few other horses on the property. A couple of frisky hunting dogs, including Winnie, a Jack Russell terrier, are part of the welcoming committee.

As we noticed the attractively arranged fox-hunting paraphernalia in the tack room, which also serves as the inn's foyer, Sandra explained, "Everything is where it is because it has a purpose. This is a home, not an inn that has been decorated."

As we were shown from room to room, each one filled with family memorabilia, we learned that the original part of the inn started as a pre-Revolutionary farmhouse. Step down into the living room, where soft leather couches, exposed hand-hewn wooden beams, and Oriental carpets provide a friendly atmosphere. A grand piano and shelves of books offer plenty of entertainment for a rainy day.

The inn has six eclectic bedrooms in the main building and two cottages up the hill. For total privacy, stay in the Spring House, the cottage in the middle of the paddock. We find it charming that the horses can come up to the porch, which has the best views of the hills. On the first floor there is a Mission oak sofa covered with pillows, a horsehair chair, and a table with legs carved to look like hunting dogs. Amenities include a VCR and TV, a selection of tapes and magazines, a radio, woodstove, refrigerator stocked with beverages, and coffee pot. Steep stairs lead to the sleeping loft, a small room with a peaked ceiling and a queen-size bed.

The Hill House Cottage, which also has a porch with a good view, is across the drive from the main house. The bedroom/living room has a double bed, Franklin stove, an easy chair, and the same amenities as in the Spring House. The ceiling has exposed beams and the roof is tin, which makes nice sounds when it rains. A spacious bathroom with a double Jacuzzi is the highlight of the cottage.

The newly built Uncle Sim Wright Suite is in the main building. One room has a high queen-size 1840 bed with posts that are at least seven feet tall. Across from the bed is a fireplace. An adjoining living room opens onto a porch. Helen's Room, an airy space with windows on three sides, is a favorite because it has a porch with a view of the hills, a fireplace, and an extra-long double bed. The sink in this bathroom once claimed residence in the White House. The Attic Room has a peaked tin ceiling and a deck from which there is a great view; the bathroom, however, is the smallest in the house and the antique bathtub is in the bedroom. Nicholson, the largest room at thirty feet long, is on the lower level of the inn and has a low ceiling. Furnishings include a piano, Franklin stove, king-size bed, and a bath with an oversize tub.

Sandra will take guests out for a two-hour trail ride. These rides, which can include jumping and cantering up the mountains, are a great way to experience the scenic vistas of this part of Virginia. Accomplished riders should ask about fox hunting. Automobile buffs will enjoy Norman's collection of restored 1960s-vintage English cars, which he is happy to show off to interested guests.

Guests can arrange ahead of time to have a seven-course dinner served before the fireplace in the formal dining room. It includes sherry and hors d'oeuvres, soup, salad, pasta, a choice of seven entrées, sorbet, and a rich chocolate dessert. Red and white wine are served with the entrée, and port is served with the coffee following the dinner.

Breakfast is served family-style outside on the deck during the warmer months or in the dining room the rest of the year. It includes juice, a fruit platter, cheese strata, French toast and bacon, or pancakes with sausage and apple stuffing.

Five rooms with private bath, $100–$150; one suite, $195; two cottages, $160–$170. All rooms have a fireplace or stove. Full breakfast and afternoon tea included; dinner, by prior arrangement only, $135 per couple, all inclusive. Children over 12 welcome in all rooms; younger children allowed in the cottages except during the fall foliage season. Third person in the room, $25 additional. Pets that don't shed are permitted in the cottages and the Summer Kitchen Room, $30 additional. Slate Mills Road, Sperryville, VA 22740; (703) 987-8025.

Where to Dine. One of the finest restaurants on the East Coast is The Inn at Little Washington (see page 157). The food-critic elite have all eaten here, and each one has rhapsodized over the experience. You can start with carpaccio of baby lamb, foie gras sautéed with ham, chilled grilled figs with ham, or lobster Napoleon with caviar. Entrées might include filet of beef served on a tangle of tart greens; grilled lobster with orzo; peppered tuna and swordfish grilled rare; or three veal medallions, each served a different way—with a purée of black olives, with sun-dried tomatoes and pesto, and in a minestrone broth. The desserts are equally extravagant. In early spring the rhubarb mousse is special, but we also recommend the unusual grapefruit pecan chocolate tart.

For lunch or a less expensive dinner, we like Four and Twenty Blackbirds in nearby Flint Hill (703-675-1111). The first floor has about half a dozen tables and three booths, and the downstairs room has low ceilings and stone walls. On our last visit, entrées included eggplant carriage wheels (slices of eggplant filled with a ricotta mixture, rolled, sliced, and served with linguine); grilled chicken with Oriental plum sauce and toasted walnuts; and broiled salmon with creamy tomato-basil sauce.

What to Do. Sperryville is a sleepy little village with a blinking yellow light marking the main intersection. There are a number of antique and curio shops in and around town, and fruit stands along the back roads in the surrounding countryside. Take a drive through the 195,000-acre Shenandoah National Park and enjoy its hiking trails, nature walks, waterfalls, and some of the finest vistas in the East. Watch the start of a fox hunt. Go to the point-to-point or steeplechase races, which are held on spring and fall weekends. Tour the large plantation homes such as Oatlands or Morven Park. Visit the impressive stalagmite and stalactite formations at Luray Caverns. Wine lovers will find much to appreciate in the growing number of Virginia vineyards: Naked Mountain Vineyards in Markham, Linden Vineyards in Linden, and Oasis Vineyard in Hume are a few favorites. Visit a shiitake mushroom farm or Berryville's Holy Cross Abbey, home of Trappist monks who bake and supply bread to the area's supermarkets. Go antiquing or simply stroll the quiet sidewalks of a secluded historic village like Waterford, Virginia.

How to Get There. From Washington, take I-495 to Route 66 west. Exit on Route 29 south to Warrenton. Go west on Route 211 to Sperryville. Turn left at the Sperryville Emporium and left again at the blinking light onto Route 522. Turn right onto Route 231, drive south eight miles, make a left onto Route 707 and proceed .6 mile to the inn.

JANE STAUFFER

Prospect Hill, *Trevilians, Virginia*

The large, circa-1732 yellow-clapboard manor house set among soaring tulip and beech trees stands at the end of an imposing 500-foot drive that's lined with a continuous hedgerow of hundred-year-old boxwoods. The outbuildings that flank the manor house at this forty-acre plantation date from 1699 to 1880. All have been preserved, and many have been converted into deluxe guest cottages. The inn has been owned by the Sheehan family since 1977. The night we stayed we met the chef, Michael Sheehan, at the innkeeper's reception.

Choose your room according to the features you prefer. Do you want to stay in the manor house or in a private cottage? Is it important to have an outside deck or patio? Do you want a double Jacuzzi? Do you want a large bedroom with a fireplace or a suite with a separate sitting area that could accommodate a third person? Twelve of the thirteen rooms and suites have wood-burning fireplaces.

Sanco Pansy's Cottage is the most popular honeymoon cottage, since it's farthest from the manor house. This cottage has a cozy feeling, a curved wood-paneled high ceiling, and a brick wall with a fireplace that faces the queen-size bed. An adjoining small sitting room has a stereo tape deck; the bath has a high ceiling with a double Jacuzzi; the front porch offers magnificent views over the fields.

The Carriage House suite, one of the outbuildings, is our favorite accommodation. It has an exposed beam ceiling and two walls with floor-to-ceiling windows that give the room an airy, impressively spacious feeling. The queen-size spool bed faces the fireplace. The house also has a separate sitting area, a patio, and a bath with a double Jacuzzi.

The sitting room in The Overseer's Cottage has lots of windows and is just as big as the bedroom, which has a queen-size bed, a fireplace, and easy chairs. The bath has a double Jacuzzi.

Two of the cottages have a more rustic feel. The cooking for the plantation was done in the Summer Kitchen until the 1920s. Now this single-room cottage has a double bed, a large fireplace set into the brick wall, which is decorated with copper pots and baskets, and a double Jacuzzi. The 1699 Boy's Log Cabin is a single small room with log walls, a fireplace, and a hard-rope double bed. The double Jacuzzi is in a particularly spacious room with a high ceiling.

We stayed in the best room in the manor house, the spacious Overton Room, which has a high queen-size four-poster bed, a fireplace, a small balcony, and a bath with a double Jacuzzi. The Terrill Room, also in the manor house, has a queen-size bed, a fireplace, and a bath with a single Jacuzzi and hand-held shower.

The Sheehans have thought of the extras that we particularly appreciate. Most rooms have refrigerators and electric coffee makers. A basket of apples, raisins, chocolate-chip cookies, and a half bottle of Virginia wine is left in each room. What more romantic way to start your visit than to uncork the wine, then light the fire . . .

Before dinner, guests gather for a glass of wine or cider with Michael Sheehan. All guests are seated at the same time at individual tables. A single four-course dinner is served. Should you have dietary restrictions, the staff willingly makes adjustments with advance notice.

The menu is based on French Provençal cooking, as Mrs. Sheehan is a native of that region of France. The night we dined we had *soupe au pistou,* a hearty tomato broth with macaroni; homemade French bread; a salad of Boston lettuce and radicchio; chicken breast with boursin cheese and a rich tomato sauce; and for dessert, a rich chocolate pâté with raspberry sauce. Other popular entrées are tournedos with shiitake mushrooms and bordelaise sauce; breast of duckling with raspberry sauce; and veal medallions with champagne mushroom sauce.

Ten rooms, $180–$250; three suites, $280; all with private bath. Tea, full breakfast, and dinner for two included. 10% discount Monday through Thursday except in April and October. Gratuities are at the discretion of the guests (10% of total rate suggested). Two-night minimum on most weekends. Children welcome in some of the cottages; under age 10, $20; over 10, $40 additional. No pets. Swimming pool and conference facilities. Route 3, Box 430, Trevilians, VA 23093; (800) 277-0844 or (703) 967-0844.

What to Do. Much of what you see as you travel through the valleys and over the hills in the Charlottesville area has been influenced by Thomas Jefferson, author of the Declaration of Independence, third president of the United States, and founder of the University of Virginia. Thomas Jefferson's home at Monticello, which he designed and took more than forty years to complete, is one of the architectural gems of America and is not to be missed. In Charlottesville, don't miss the rotunda at the University of Virginia, designed by Jefferson and modeled after the Pantheon in Rome. Sample the local wines and see where they're made: We like the Vin Gris de Pinot Noir at Simeon, the Merlot Reserve at Montdomaine, and the Cabernet Sauvignon at Barboursville. Drive part of the Blue Ridge Parkway; take a walking tour of historic Lexington including the Marshall Museum, Lee Chapel, and Stonewall Jackson's home. Visit Woodrow Wilson's birthplace and the Museum of American Frontier Culture in Staunton.

How to Get There. From Charlottesville take I-64 east to exit 27. Take Route 15 south to Zion Crossroads. Turn left on Route 250 east. Go 1 mile to Route 613; turn left and continue for 3 miles to the inn.

JANE STAUFFER

Williamsburg Inn, *Williamsburg, Virginia*

From the moment you drive up to the front entrance of this formal, whitewashed, landscaped, brick world-class hotel and are greeted by friendly staff, you know you have arrived at someplace special. Williamsburg is a must-see for visiting dignitaries, and many of the political movers and shakers of the world have stayed or dined at the inn.

The Rockefellers, who were involved in the intimate design and furnishing of the hotel, chose the Regency period to contrast with the Colonial restoration of the town. All of the rooms have wall-to-wall carpeting, coordinating lined draperies, bedspreads, and upholstered easy chairs. Televisions are tucked into armoires; bureaus and dressing tables are reproduction antiques.

Should you want a larger room, the newer bed-sitting rooms have louvered doors that separate the sitting rooms from the large bedrooms, which have king-size beds. Other rooms we particularly like are those overlooking the golf course. For a winter visit we suggest one of the thirteen rooms with a wood-burning fireplace.

In addition to the elegant Williamsburg Inn, you can also stay in one of the restored eighteenth-century buildings located in the Colonial town. Wake up in the morning and leave your room to wander quiet streets and walk through the gardens before the day-trippers arrive. Rooms are furnished with Colonial reproductions. The Schumacher fabrics are the same as those you can purchase at the craft house or at any Williamsburg shop throughout the United States.

Most of the Colonial accommodations for couples are in the tavern rooms. We like the first-floor rooms in the Brick House tavern with windows facing Duke of Gloucester Street. For a winter visit, we'd suggest the more expensive Chiswell House tavern or The Orlando Jones House, since they each have a room with a queen-size canopy bed and a fireplace.

The Colonial houses range in size from one to four bedrooms. For a romantic stay we favor Peter Hay's Kitchen, a one-bedroom house that has a living room with a fireplace. Another good choice is the Orlando Jones Kitchen.

For a romantic dinner we suggest the Regency Room at the Williamsburg Inn. The gracious surroundings are enchantingly sophisticated, the service refined, the ambience peaceful. The upper dining room has curved red couches, large floral arrangements, and showcases filled with exquisite pieces of Oriental art. The bright and airy lower dining room overlooks the courtyard and golf course. This room is decorated in the English Regency style, with hand-painted Oriental cherry blossom panels on the walls, fluted columns, and large crystal chandeliers overhead.

Our captain deftly prepared a Caesar salad tableside with all the appropriate ingredients and proper panache. An appetizer of pasta in a cream sauce with pieces of smoked salmon was delicious. The red snapper came stuffed with crabmeat, and the scalloppine of veal was served with chunks of fresh lobster meat on a bed of leeks with melon and tomato balls and scoops of vegetables. Other entrées include roast medallions of rabbit and Gorgonzola polenta, and classic chateaubriand, carved tableside.

An impressive dessert cart included a Sacher torte, Black Forest cake, warm southern pecan bread pudding, various fresh fruit tarts, and a Governor's cake, layers of chocolate mousse and chocolate cake.

Breakfast at the Regency Room is a most civilized way to start the day, less for the menu offerings than for the subtle service details, such as the demitasse of coffee and miniature breakfast muffins offered to all guests as soon as they are seated. Our list of favorites includes the homemade granola served with cream, the thick slices of Sally Lunn French toast, and the pecan waffles served with warm syrup.

For dining in a Colonial atmosphere, the Shields, King's Arms, Chowning's, and Campbell taverns are all in the restored historic district.

The Williamsburg Inn has 80 rooms, $205–$279, and 22 suites, $335–$625. Includes afternoon tea in the East Lounge, but not breakfast. Children welcome, $12 additional. No pets. Located on Francis Street. The Colonial Taverns and Houses have 85 rooms and suites. Rooms, $99–$199, depending on the room and time of year. One-bedroom houses, $157–$296. Full breakfast at the Shields Tavern and afternoon tea at the Market Square Tavern included. Children welcome. The Regency Room serves breakfast 7:30 to 10 A.M., $10–$15; lunch, 12 to 2 P.M., $8.75–$13.75; and dinner, 6:30 to 9:30 P.M., entrées, $19-$32. Box B, Williamsburg, VA 23187; (800) HISTORY.

What to Do. Walk through the historic district, visiting the workshops and talking to the craftspeople who practice eighteenth-century trades—the silversmith, gunsmith, wheelwright, and wigmaker. Stop for lunch in one of the taverns. Tour the Governor's Palace and the capitol. Major museums include the Wallace Gallery, with more than 8,000 decorative objects from the Colonial period and the newly expanded Abby Aldrich Folk Art Center. Visit the plantation home at Carter's Grove. Sports facilities on the inn grounds include two sixteen-hole Robert Trent Jones golf courses, a fully equipped fitness center, eight tennis courts, swimming pools, croquet, and lawn bowling.

How to Get There. From Washington take I-95 south. Take I-295 around Richmond, then take I-64 to Williamsburg. Follow signs to the historic district and the Williamsburg Inn.

JANE STAUFFER

The Swag, *Waynesville, North Carolina*

The approach to this mountain-top lodge is an adventure in itself. After climbing several thousand feet for more than six miles on a two-lane rural road, guests turn onto a private gravel mountain road that continues for another 2.5 miles and rises still another thousand feet to a 5,000-foot elevation. And what do you expect to find at this altitude?

We found peace and solitude on hundreds of acres along a mountain ridge. The Great Smoky Mountains National Park,

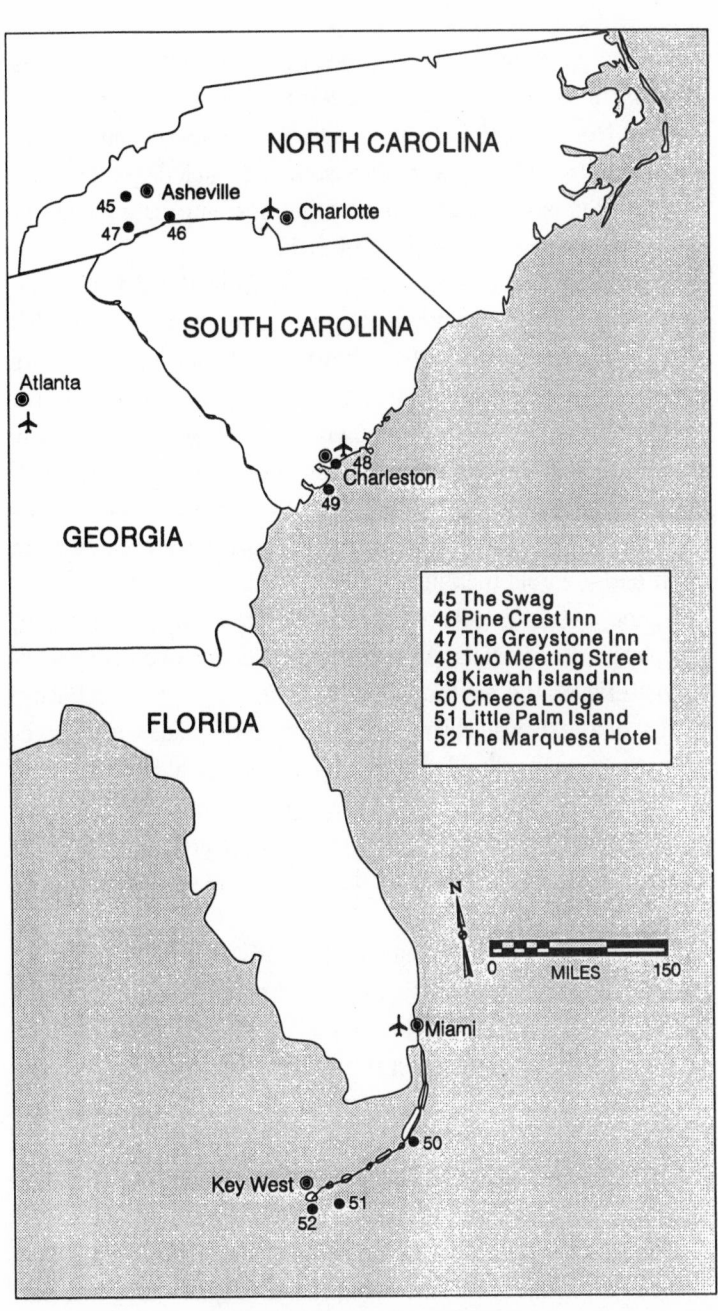

45 The Swag
46 Pine Crest Inn
47 The Greystone Inn
48 Two Meeting Street
49 Kiawah Island Inn
50 Cheeca Lodge
51 Little Palm Island
52 The Marquesa Hotel

with miles of hiking trails, borders the property. The inn was made from five log-and-stone buildings that were collected by owners Deener and Dan Matthews in Tennessee and North Carolina. The buildings were disassembled, hauled up the mountain, and combined to make one of the most interesting country inns we have had the privilege of visiting.

The compound centerpiece is made from the 200-year-old Lonesome Valley Primitive Baptist Church from Hancock County, Tennessee. The hand-hewn logs (including 36-footers that span the cathedral ceiling of the living room) and the massive rock fireplace are living testaments to the skill of the early settlers, and of the modern-day craftspeople, who put the buildings back together. The sofas, draperies, and dining-room tables were made by a Tennessee native. Lamps were created from birch bark and old milk jugs.

In the evening, guests can enjoy a working player piano, complete with 150 rolls. An extensive collection of current reading material on the Southern Appalachians ranges from scholarly works of the Appalachian people to nature guides and large-format picture books. There is also a theological library on the premises and videotapes that Dan, the minister of Trinity Episcopal Church in New York City, has made. Dan spends only his vacation and some long weekends here; Deener is the innkeeper throughout the season.

The rooms are all furnished differently and decorated with style. The rough wood walls, exposed beams, and bare floors contrast with coordinated bedspreads, pillows, and area rugs. Other features include small refrigerators, hair-dryers, magnifying mirrors, and steam showers in some of the rooms, fireplaces or stoves in others. Some of the rooms have private balconies; others have sleeping lofts. Most rooms have queen-size beds.

The most romantic accommodation is a spacious, newly built two-room cabin. The living room has a fireplace and wet bar, and the bedroom has a king-size bed. There is a private back deck and a bath with steam shower and a two-person whirlpool tub. The Woodshed, another cabin smaller than the other, has a living room with a fireplace, sofa bed and refrigerator, a bedroom with a queen-size bed, and a bath with a tub and shower.

Room C-4 is the best room in the lodge, a corner room with a queen-size bed, a fireplace, refrigerator, a bath with a shower and whirlpool tub with a view of the mountains, and a private balcony. Equally popular is room 3-2, a corner room with a queen-size bed, fireplace, refrigerator, steam shower, and private balcony.

And how will you dine at the Swag? Guests sit on cane ladderback chairs at two long tables. Grace is said before dinner. Because this is a "dry county," the inn cannot sell liquor, but guests are welcome to bring their own. Our delicious dinner included fruit salad with poppyseed dressing, chicken breasts teriyaki with water chestnuts, couscous, mixed squash, red peppers and pecans, and orange muffins. Dessert was angel-food cake with lemon icing. Breakfast included juice, granola, fresh peaches, French toast, and sausage. If you'll be away from the inn at lunchtime, Deener prepares good trail lunches.

If the weather is poor, guests need only go to the basement of Chestnut Lodge where, believe it or not, there is a regulation-size racquetball court and a sauna, both totally underground. When the weather is pleasant there is croquet and badminton, and a swinging bridge and miles of trails that lead from the inn into the Great Smoky Mountains National Park to explore.

Open late May through October. Twelve rooms and two cabins, ten with fireplace or woodstoves, each with private bath. Weekends and the month of October, $175–$290 for two, including all three meals. Midweek, $150–$275. Children of all ages welcome. Third person in the room, $60. 15% service charge is additional. Two-night minimum stay. Route 2, Box 280-A, Waynesville, NC 28786; (704) 926-0430.

What to Do.   You can easily spend your days at The Swag hiking the Great Smoky Mountains National Park trails that start at the property or immersing yourself in the owners' extensive library of southern culture. If you want to come down from the mountain you can drive less than an hour to Asheville and tour the 250-room Biltmore Mansion, the largest private home in America. Completed in 1895 by George Vanderbilt, whose elder brothers built the Breakers and the Marble House in Newport, Rhode Island, the main building is reached via a winding three-mile road through a grand hardwood and pine forest. The interior is furnished with tapestries, chandeliers, and furniture collected in Europe. There is a 72-by-48-foot Gothic banquet hall with an arched ceiling 75 feet high. The property, which encompasses thousands of acres, includes gardens and a winery. From Asheville, drive the Blue Ridge Parkway to Cherokee, the main entrance to the Great Smoky Mountains National Park, where you can get information on hiking trails and ranger-led walks and talks. Visit the Museum of the Cherokee Indian and the Qualla Arts and Crafts Mutual for an introduction to the Cherokee Indians and authentic Indian crafts. If you are interested in fine crafts visit Penland School northeast of Asheville, one of the top craft schools in the country, and then visit some of the artists' studios and galleries in the area.

How to Get There.   From Asheville, take exit 20 off I-40 west, go south on Route 276 for 2.8 miles, turn right on Hemphill Road, travel about four miles to the inn's private road.

The Twain Cottage

Pine Crest Inn, *Tryon, North Carolina*

Twenty-two wood-burning fireplaces scattered throughout this ten-building complex, along with a large, well-stocked library of current titles (most of which have been read by the innkeepers) and a first-rate restaurant makes Pine Crest Inn a destination in itself. Jeremy and Jennifer Wainwright have given this seventy-year-old complex a complete facelift, yet have preserved the architectural integrity of the main inn (which is on the National Register of Historic Places) and the fieldstone and log country cabins situated among three landscaped acres of large pines, giant oaks, and flowering dogwood. Seventeen of the twenty-eight rooms have been totally redesigned within the last five years. Some have the Ralph Lauren equestrian look. And why not? Tryon (population 4,000), located in the foothills of the Blue Ridge Mountains, is in the middle of horse country with a full complement of shows, hunts, steeplechase races, and the horsy set.

The Fitzgerald Suite in the Twain Cottage, converted from an old log cabin, is one of our favorites. Its spacious living room has a massive contemporary-style leather couch and two leather easy chairs (the kind you melt into) that face a large stone fireplace and stone wall. The ceiling has exposed beams. Wall-to-wall carpeting extends from the living room to the bedroom, where there is a king-size bed, a second stone fireplace, and matching maroon wing-back chairs.

Swayback Cabin, a 200-year-old log cabin surrounded by pine trees, is the most private of all the cabins. Its single room has a queen-size bed, fireplace, loveseat, a small bath with a shower only, and a stone patio.

The oversize Windsor Room is another honeymoon favorite, decorated with floral patterns, lace, a crystal chandelier, two loveseats near the fireplace, and a king-size bed.

The White Oak Suite has fireplaces in the bedroom, which has a four-poster king-size bed, and in the living room. This suite also has two full baths.

On the second floor of the main house we like the Pine Room, which has a queen-size bed with a paisley canopy and dark-green corduroy headboard, a matching sofa, and cherry wood–paneled walls.

The corner Gold Room, also with cherry paneling, is down the hall. We immediately noticed the framed Audubon flamingo print hung over the fireplace, which is surrounded by bright red tiles. This room has a queen-size bed and two comfortable matching easy chairs perfectly coordinated to pick up the orangy color of the flamingo.

A full breakfast, served from 8 to 9:30 A.M., gives a choice of virtually anything a guest could want. It includes freshly squeezed orange juice; cereal (hot or cold, including homemade granola); eggs Benedict or Florentine; omelets with any combination of ham, cheese, mushrooms, and other fillings; pancakes or waffles with fruit and nut toppings; plus bacon, sausage, grits, toast, and muffins.

There is a large stone wood-burning fireplace in the main

dining room. The old barnboard and plaster walls are decorated with china plates, old lanterns, shiny copper pots, and in one discreet corner, the Wainwrights' wonderful collection of Holbein pencil drawings. The waiters were trained in the Old Southern Railroad Pullman-car style of service—and several have been at the inn for more than thirty years.

We started our dinner with a fine seafood gumbo. The mountain trout, supplied by a local farm, was served deboned, split in half and grilled, a beautiful and tasty preparation. The crabcakes served with traditional tartar sauce on the side were as fine as any, with little filler and no discernible bits of shell. An excellent roasted rack of lamb was seasoned with Dijon mustard and served with a Madeira and mint sauce.

Thirty rooms and suites, all with private bath, $95–$130. Continental breakfast is included. Children of all ages welcome; under 12, $10 additional. No pets. Dinner served Monday through Thursday, 6 to 8:30 P.M., Friday and Saturday, 6 to 9:15 P.M. Entrées, $14–$23. Pine Crest Lane, Tryon, NC 28782; (800) 633-3001 or (704) 859-9135.

What to Do. Drive less than an hour north to Asheville and tour the 250-room Biltmore Mansion, the largest private home in America. It was completed in 1895 by George Vanderbilt, whose elder brothers built the Breakers and the Marble House in Newport, Rhode Island. The main building is reached via a winding three-mile road through a grand hardwood and pine forest. The interior is furnished with tapestries, chandeliers, and furniture collected in Europe. There is a 72-by-48-foot Gothic banquet hall with an arched ceiling 75 feet high. The property, which encompasses thousands of acres, includes gardens and a winery.

From Asheville take the Blue Ridge Parkway to Cherokee, the main entrance to Great Smoky Mountains National Park, where you can get information on hiking trails and ranger-led walks and talks. Visit the Museum of the Cherokee Indian and the Qualla Arts and Crafts Mutual for an introduction to the Cherokee Indians and the best authentic Indian crafts in the area. If you are interested in fine crafts you should plan to visit Penland School northeast of Asheville, one of the top craft schools in the country, and then visit some of the artists' studios and galleries in the area.

How to Get There.   From Asheville take I-26 south to Tryon, which is just north of the North Carolina/South Carolina border.

JANE STAUFFER

The Greystone Inn, *Lake Toxaway, North Carolina*

If you're looking for a deluxe lakeside resort with a full range of outdoor activities, this is a good place to go. The refurbished 1915 mansion situated on the banks of 640-acre Lake Toxaway, the largest private lake in North Carolina, has nineteen luxurious accommodations on six levels.

The Presidential Suite, created from the mansion's former library, is the ultimate in luxury. The king-size bed, set in front of a wall of windows overlooking the lake, is dwarfed by the expanse of this enormous room, which has a twenty-five-foot ceiling with exposed oak beams, a massive stone fireplace, and matching upholstered chintz-covered chaise longue, couch, easy chairs, and draperies. There is a double marble Jacuzzi and a separate room with a full bath. The old library's magazine room, which you reach by climbing a set of circular stairs, is now a sleeping loft with two twin beds.

In the mansion, guests can choose between standard-size rooms with queen-size beds, deluxe larger rooms with a queen, king, or two double beds, and the more spacious luxury rooms, some of which have balconies, fireplaces, oversize Jacuzzis, and outstanding views. You can't go wrong with any of the rooms; all have high-quality furnishings and fabrics, and even the smaller rooms have access to all common areas and facilities. We stayed in the Moltz Room, the old master bedroom. It has a queen-size bed, fireplace, and a bath large enough to be a separate room, with an oversize Jacuzzi and a double sink. The Heinitsh Room on the first floor has a queen-size bed, fireplace, sitting area, and a private entrance leading to a stone terrace. The Firestone Room has a private entrance and a terrace overlooking Lake Toxaway. Other features include a king-size bed, large stone fireplace, and the original black iron stove once used for canning.

Another option is to stay in Hillmont, a newly constructed building twenty-five feet from the lake with twelve spacious units each about 650 square feet. Each room has an unobstructed view of the lake and a private deck not visible from any other room. Being able to sip a cup of coffee on your deck in the early morning, dressed only in a terrycloth robe, is the ultimate in privacy. Each room in this building has a gas fireplace, a wet bar, shower, and oversize Jacuzzi. The two best rooms in this building are the Lupton Room and the Astor Room, both corner rooms on the upper level, with king-size beds and cathedral ceilings.

Outstanding cuisine is served in the dining room, which overlooks the water. The six-course menu changes daily but always includes a choice of appetizer, soup, entrée, and dessert. Remember to bring your own wine since this is a dry county. There is no cork fee.

The night we dined, we had alligator fritters in spicy tomato sauce and a cold plate of sliced duck and *andouille* (cajun smoked pork) and venison sausages as a first course, followed by mushroom barley and French onion soup. A plate of smoked North Carolina trout and smoked salmon is another appetizer often on the menu. The lamb chops were two double ribs, perfectly cooked and served with cherry chutney. Other choices were red snapper with a pecan caper sauce and chicken breasts coated with crushed macadamia nuts. Pan-fried trout stuffed with jumbo lump crabmeat and topped with béarnaise sauce is one of the most popular entrées. For dessert, we recommend the sour-cream chocolate peanut-butter pie, strawberries Romanoff, or the homemade ice cream.

All of the sports activities are included in the rates except for golf fees at the exclusive country club located next to the inn. If you can arrange to stay mid-week during May, both the greens fees and the cart are included. Mid-week rates during June and September include the greens fees. There is no charge for use of the paddleboats, canoes, Sunfish, Windsurfer, and electric-powered boat; water skiing and instruction or tennis and swimming. The owner, Tim Lovelace, usually takes guests on a sunset party cruise (on Saturday night, champagne and hors d'oeuvres are served; soda served on other days).

At Thanksgiving, Christmas, and New Year's, celebrations at the inn include organized hikes, a champagne tasting, casino night, and activities for children.

Open April through New Year's weekend. Thirty rooms and

two lakeside cottage suites, all with private baths, $250–$330. Presidential Suite, $420. Rates are for two people and include full breakfast, high tea, dinner, tennis, swimming, boating, and lake cruise. Sunday through Thursday, five-night vacation packages available. Lower rates in April and mid-week during May, November, and December. Children welcome. Infants, no charge; 1 to 5 years, $25; 6 to 10 years, $50; 11 and up, $70 additional. No pets. 15% service charge is additional. Greystone Lane, Lake Toxaway, NC 28747; (704) 966-4700. Outside North Carolina, (800) 824-5766.

What to Do.   You can easily spend your entire time at the inn taking advantage of the golf, tennis, boating, and swimming. Arrange for a picnic lunch and enjoy it at one of three secluded waterfalls located on the property, at the top of the mountain overlooking Lake Toxaway, or out on the lake on the electric whisper craft. One of the best whitewater rafting trips in the East is on the Chattooga River, about an hour away. From the inn, drive north about 35 minutes to the Blue Ridge Parkway. Head west on the parkway to the Great Smoky Mountains National Park and east to the Biltmore House in Asheville. Both Asheville and the Smoky Mountains are about an hour's drive.

How to Get There.   From Asheville take I-26 south to Route 64. Take Route 64 west through Hendersonville and Brevard to Lake Toxaway. A detailed map showing the location of the inn is available at the guard house at the entrance to the lake.

Two Meeting Street, *Charleston, South Carolina*

The area of Charleston, south of Broad Street next to the Battery and the White Point Gardens, is the most exclusive residential area of the city. This magnificent Victorian home, completed in 1892, is built in the Queen Anne style with fish-scale turrets, stained-glass windows, and curved piazzas. Since 1946, the inn has been owned by members of the Spell family; the current innkeeper is Karen Spell.

The first floor, including the ten-foot doors, is paneled with carved English oak. Two of the nine stained-glass windows are by Tiffany. The dining room has a spectacular sunburst stained-glass window over a six-foot carved oak china cupboard that's filled with crystal. Guests can have their breakfast in this room surrounded by the family's elegant silver and fine china collections. The common rooms are sumptuously decorated with family pieces such as an eleven-floor étagère in the Renaissance Revival style and an antique English Chippendale mahogany chest with satin-wood inlay. Original artwork by renowned bird painter Anne Worsham Richardson, a Charleston artist, is prominently displayed.

Guests enjoy afternoon sherry in the living room or on one of the piazzas that overlook the Battery, and watch the continual parade of horse-drawn tourist carriages that stop in front of the inn for photographs and commentary.

Room 2 is the most popular room since it has both a gas fireplace and access to the porch; it generally is booked seven months ahead for the weekends. The room has a queen-size canopy bed with a curved tester and a curved turret window that overlooks the street.

Room 4 is another top choice. This room is the same size as the dining room below it. Special features include luxurious coordinated wallpaper and fabrics, a curved wall with windows, two double beds, and a large bath with a marble sink and a five-foot Victorian tub.

Room 5 has windows on three sides, a window seat, gas fireplace, and a tiny balcony that looks out over the rooftops of Charleston. This room also has a large bath with a marble sink and a five-foot Victorian tub. Note: Most of the Victorian tubs have hand-held shower attachments.

Room 3 has a queen-size canopy bed, a bath with a shower only, and access to the second-floor porch. Room 9, the original music room, is on the first floor. It has a queen-size canopy bed and an armoire. The three third-floor rooms are smaller, have standard-height slanted ceilings, and do not have the same Victorian ambiance as the rooms on the first and second floors. Be sure to plan way ahead, since the best rooms are usually booked months in advance.

Nine rooms, all with private bath. First- and second-floor rooms, $135–$155; third-floor rooms, $90–$105. Children over 8 welcome; $20 additional for third person in room. Continental breakfast included. Two-night minimum stay on weekend. No pets. No smoking. No credit cards. 2 Meeting Street at the Battery, Charleston, SC 29401; (803) 723-7322.

Where to Dine. Million, a classic French restaurant, is the height of decadence (2 Unity Alley; 803-577-7472). The preparation, the service, the food, and the decor are superb. Entrées we sampled included lightly breaded sea scallops with a touch of herbed mousse in the middle of each, accompanied by St. John's Island baby okra. Mackerel was served with sliced artichoke hearts and clams.

At Louis's Charleston Grill (Omni Hotel, 224 King Street; 803-577-4522), diners can graze through the collection of appetizers and sample the soups, such as grouper chowder with saffron onions or brown oyster stew with benne seeds.

The raised horseshoe-shaped bar in the center of the main dining room at Magnolias (185 East Bay Street; 803-577-7771) is usually packed with trendy Charlestonians. Our waiter suggested the tasty yellow grits cakes, which were seared on a skillet and covered with tasso gravy made with chicken stock, cream, parsley, and bits of spicy Cajun ham.

What to Do. There is an excitement, a warmth and friendliness about this city that give it a feeling far different from other historic places. The best time to visit is March and April during the Historic Charleston Foundation Festival of Houses and Gardens, when more than 100 private homes, gardens, and churches are open for guided tours. Come in early June for the Spoleto Arts Festival, which includes more than 100 performances of classical ballet, modern dance, opera, chamber music, symphonic and choral concerts, jazz, and theater, along with visual arts exhibitions throughout the city. Walk the historic streets, smell the aroma of boxwood and sweet bay in the narrow alleys, peek through the ornamental wrought-iron gates to catch glimpses of manicured gardens, and stroll along the Battery as the sun sets. Purchase a basket from the sweetgrass basketmakers who come from the South Carolina Sea Islands. Take a tour boat to Fort Sumter to see where the Civil War began. Spend a day touring the plantations and historic homes located outside the city, including Drayton Hall, Magnolia Plantation and Gardens, and Middleton Place. Golfers will want to play one of the four courses on Kiawah Island or two at Wild Dunes Resort.

How to Get There. Take I-95 south to I-26. When the road ends take Meeting Street to the Battery at the tip of Charleston. The inn is on your left just before White Point Gardens.

View from a room at the inn

Kiawah Island Inn, *Kiawah Island, South Carolina*

The combination of four golf courses, ten miles of pristine, noncommercial beaches, a variety of dining options, and rooms that overlook the ocean make this lushly landscaped resort a rare idyllic island paradise. Kiawah Island is located twenty-one miles south of Charleston and is easily accessible by car. Hurricane Hugo did not cause the damage to the trees here that you will still see elsewhere in the area. What we like about the resort is that you can spend your time at the beach, pools, tennis courts, or on one of the golf courses in relative seclusion. You are not locked into a meal plan and so you can eat at whatever restaurant you wish or, if you stay in one of the villas, you also can do your own cooking.

Guests have the option of staying at the Kiawah Island Inn or renting a villa. The large inn rooms are clustered in four buildings. The more expensive rooms, which we like the best, have views of the water from the decks. Rooms 213, 313, 226, and 326 are the far corner rooms closest to the water in each of the two inn buildings that have ocean views. The other two buildings are in a more wooded setting and overlook the lagoons. Each room has two double beds or a king-size bed, a refrigerator, television, telephone, and private balcony overlooking the ocean, the sand dunes, or the tropical forests. Walkways to the pools and dining room are lined with masses of flowers and plants.

There are 300 privately owned villas (condominiums) and cottages on the property, some with oceanfront views and others set in the marshes or next to the lagoons. The six-story oceanfront Windswept Building offers two- and three-bedroom villas equipped with a full kitchen, washer/dryer, and screened deck. The top floors offer incredible panoramic views.

If you are a golfer, there are four great courses to choose from. The newest is the Ocean Course, the site of the Ryder Cup Matches in 1991, located at the tip of the island with dramatic ocean vistas on every hole. It has been named by *Golf Magazine* as one of the top 100 courses in the world. For tennis enthusiasts there are 28 Har-Tru clay and hard courts. Bicyclists have fourteen miles of trails and strollers have the ten miles of beaches to explore. There are three swimming pools at the inn and two additional pools at other locations on the island.

Marine biologists and naturalists lead Kiawah Kollege environmental experiences such as ocean seining with dragnets, loggerhead sea turtle preservation, bird watching, and nature walks through lagoons, creeks, rivers, and ocean environments.

There are four restaurants on the island. The Jasmine Porch is the restaurant at the Kiawah Island Inn. Reserve a table next to the large windows that overlook the colorful gardens, the dunes, and the Atlantic Ocean. We started our dinner with an exceptionally good mildly spiced seafood sausage of shrimp, crab, and scallops wrapped in crisp layers of phyllo dough, accompanied by a red bell-pepper cream sauce and thin griddle corncakes topped with pulled (shredded) Carolina barbecue pork.

The salmon filet entrée, covered with crisp baked shoestring potatoes and served with a light sorrel sauce, was a pretty and tasty contrast of colors and textures. Other choices included pan-seared sea scallops with a fresh basil, cilantro, and tomato butter sauce, and grilled smoked pork porterhouse steak served with apple-walnut butter and five-vegetable slaw. We shared a traditional napoleon covered with hot caramel sauce for dessert.

The impressive Sunday brunch buffet features ice sculptures, a wok station for stir-frys, waffles and pancakes made to order, eggs Benedict, speckled heart grits (coarser than traditional grits), smoked fish, and other Low Country specials. The highlight of the week is the Mingo Point Barbecue and Oyster Roast held each Saturday night during the summer.

One hundred fifty inn rooms, $110–$220. Three hundred one- to four-bedroom villas. One bedroom, $110–$265; two to four bedrooms, $155–$435. Weekly rates available in the villas. Lower rates in the winter. Swimming pool. Fees for golf, tennis, bicycles, tours, children's activities, environmental experiences. Meals available but not included. The Jasmine Porch is open daily for breakfast; lunch, 11:30 A.M. to 2:30 P.M., $6–$11.95; dinner, 6 to 10 P.M., entrées, $11.95–$22.95. Sunday brunch (mid-April through October), $19.95. Children welcome. No pets. Mailing address: P.O. Box 12357, Charleston, SC 29422-2357; (800) 654-2924 or (803) 768-2121.

What to Do.   There are four golf courses, including the new ocean course used for the Ryder Cup tournaments; twenty-eight tennis courts; and ten miles of pristine sand beach. Rent bicycles and explore the fourteen miles of roads on the island. Sailboats and Windsurfers can also be rented. Kiawah Kollege offers hands-on environmental activities. Take a day trip into Charleston. Walk the historic streets, smell the aroma of boxwood and sweet bay in the narrow alleys, peek through the ornamental wrought-iron gates to catch glimpses of manicured gardens, and stroll along the Battery as the sun sets. Purchase a basket from the sweetgrass basketmakers who come from the South Carolina Sea Islands. Take the tour boat to Fort Sumter. Spend a day touring the plantations.

How to Get There.   Take I-95 south to I-26. When the road ends, turn right on Route 17, left on Route 700, and left on Bohicket Road to Kiawah Island. The airport is a 45-minute drive northwest. Rental cars and airport shuttle service are available.

Cheeca Lodge, *Islamorada, Florida*

Sitting on our screened-in terrace we could see the moon casting a long beam across the Atlantic Ocean and could make out the shape of the 525-foot-long fishing pier, perfect for an evening stroll. The sounds of a warm sea breeze rustled through the leaves of the coconut palms. After an exquisite dinner at this understated, elegant resort, we decided that this was an ideal way to end the day.

This deluxe complex, built on twenty-seven acres, has recently undergone a $33-million expansion and renovation. Most of the accommodations are in newly constructed three-story villas and in the four-story main lodge. There is a 50-foot lap pool, a free-form pool, saltwater pool, four whirlpools, six lighted tennis courts, a scaled-down nine-hole executive golf course, and three restaurants. Water sports equipment includes Windsurfers, glass-bottom paddleboats, Hobie cats, parasails, and powerboats used for fishing, snorkeling, or scuba diving. At the end of the fishing pier is a marked underwater snorkel trail.

The rooms overlook the ocean or landscaped ponds filled with tropical fish. All of the rooms and suites are newly furnished in the English Colonial rattan look. The best accommodations are the three oceanfront suites, rooms in the oceanfront villas, and fourth-floor ocean view lodge rooms, each of which has a balcony overlooking the water. Each suite (whether ocean or island view) has a full kitchen, screened balcony with a table and chairs, bedroom with a king-size bed or two double beds, and a separate living room with a convertible couch. Other features include two televisions, a VCR, two telephones, and a fully stocked refrigerator (additional charge for items consumed). The bath includes a tiled oversized shower with glass doors, tiled floor, and a separate dressing area with a second sink. For those on a more modest budget, choose an island-view room and do your ocean-gazing from the beach chairs.

Families with children ages five through twelve can spend the day at the inn's Camp Cheeca, where they will take part in a full or half day of environmentally oriented activities such as snorkeling, observing marine life through the glass-bottom boats, and fishing. Diners at Cheeca Lodge can choose between The Atlantic's Edge, the gourmet restaurant, or the more informal outdoor Ocean Terrace restaurant, which is open only during the high season. At The Atlantic Edge the best tables are set in front of the dining room's expansive curved window with a full view of the water. Our dinner stood out as one of the finest and most unusual meals we've had in the Keys. The contrast of textures among the slightly chewy blackened corn, the lumps of crabmeat, and the rich cream of the roasted corn and lump crab soup made a particularly satisfying opener. Other appetizers included ceviche of yellow-tail snapper and steamed stone-crab potstickers.

Cheeca Lodge is setting a trend in environmental responsibility by keeping endangered species of fish off the menu. Swordfish and conch are not available, and stone crabs and lobster are being served less frequently than they once were. If you should go fishing the chef will prepare your catch—often grouper, snapper, or dolphin (the fish)—anyway you like. The Taste of Islamorada ($29) is a set dinner that changes weekly. We had an Oriental vegetable salad with crab fritters, seared duck breast on a bed of leeks, orange-flavored lobster ravioli, and a dessert of a ginger goat cheese cake in sesame phyllo crust. Two glasses of wine, one with the appetizer and another with the entrée, are included with this dinner. Other entrées are onion-crusted snapper with tomatoes and artichokes; baked grouper in plaintain crust; mixed grill of duck, lamb, and lobster with vegetables tossed in a roasted red pepper balsamic vinaigrette; and filet of beef served in a potato cage.

If you and your companion have a hearty appetite, order the sampler key lime plate to share. This dessert includes portions of a key-lime tartlet, chocolate truffle cake with key-lime sauce, and key-lime mousse. Other tempting choices are sliced mangoes with guava sorbet and chocolate sauce, or poached pears filled with chocolate mousse and chocolate-caramel sauce.

The Ocean Terrace room serve lighter fare in a tropical, open-air setting. The lunch and dinner menus are similar and include such items as tropical fruit salad with strawberry cottage cheese; spicy shrimp and crab pizza with sundried tomatoes, artichoke hearts, and shiitake mushrooms; a broiled rib-eye steak sandwich with fried onion rings; and sautéed Florida grouper.

Two hundred and three rooms and suites, all with private bath. Third week in December through third week of April, oceanview rooms and island-view suites, $275–$800, island-view rooms, $200–$475. At other times of the year, oceanview rooms and island-view suites, $200–$500, island-view rooms, $125–$325. Presidential suite, $1,025 (in season) or $700 (off-season). Children under sixteen free, extra adult, $25 additional. Meals are not included. Golf, $12; tennis, $10; Camp Cheeca, $22. Breakfast, lunch, dinner served daily. Lunch 11 A.M. to 4

P.M., $6.50–$12.50. Dinner, 5:30 to 10 P.M., (11 P.M. on Friday and Saturday), entrées, $16.75–$32. U.S. Highway 1, Mile Marker 82, Islamorada, FL 33036; (800) 327-2888 or (305) 664-4651.

What to Do. The Theater of the Sea, located on Windley Key, just north of Islamorada, includes a glass-bottom boat ride that features a wide variety of marine life, from sharks to tropical fish, and a performing dolphin show. The adventurous can even swim with these good-natured mammals. John Pennekamp Coral Reef State Park, located on Key Largo about twenty minutes away, is the only underwater park in the continental United States. It is a favorite for snorkeling or diving. There are also glass-bottom boat trips to the reef for observing tropical fish and coral formations. Everglades National Park is located sixty miles north of Islamorada. There are walking trails, canoeing, and activities led by naturalists. To get off the beaten track, take a boat ride to Lignum Vitae, home to many rare trees and plant life, some over 10,000 years old, or to Indian Keys, a historic park that has returned to its original natural state.

How to Get There. From Miami, take U.S. 1 for 82 miles south to Islamorada. The hotel can also arrange for transportation from Miami International Airport, 75 miles to the north.

JANE STAUFFER

Little Palm Island, *Little Torch Key, Florida*

This island hideaway, complete with palm trees, thatched-grass huts, hammocks, white sand, and a gourmet dining room, is a five-acre paradise. You won't be bothered with the sound of telephones, televisions, or horns. The biggest decision you'll make is what to eat at your next meal.

Guests check in at a small building just off the overseas highway at milepost 28.5 on Little Torch Key. Hostesses in dress whites take care of the paperwork for your stay, offer you a drink, and make you feel comfortable until the hourly departure of the launch, which takes 15 minutes to reach the island.

Every thatched-roof bungalow has two suites, each with a living room, bedroom, spacious bath, and outdoor deck area. Suites have a king-size bed or two double beds with colorful Caribbean print spreads. Decorative mosquito netting is draped attractively over the beds. The living rooms have a fully stocked minibar (additional charge for items consumed), and a call button for room service or emergencies (there are no telephones or televisions in the rooms). The spacious baths have a double sink, a shower, and a Jacuzzi tub. A rope hammock outside each room sets the mood for the island. We particularly liked the view from the rooms facing the Atlantic, and were delighted to hear the water and the sound of the wind through the palm trees as we lay in bed.

If you like to golf, play tennis, or spend the night on the town, this is not your island in the sun. But if sitting in the lap of luxury, fishing, snorkeling, diving, sailing, reading, and enjoying three meals a day from a first-rate kitchen is your idea of rest and relaxation, look no further.

The dining experience matches the pristine picture-perfect setting. We sat on one of the two open-air decks surrounded by palm trees and views of the ocean. A third intimate dining room has a woven mat ceiling and walls of cypress decorated with trophy fish and contemporary paintings. This is the way to relax: light classical music playing in the background, the expertise of a top Swiss chef in the kitchen, and no pressure to go someplace after dinner. The restaurant is open to the public, but guests staying on the island have priority in choosing their dining time. Bring a sweater in the evening, as the outdoor deck can get breezy.

A recent lunch on the deck overlooking the small sand beach started with cold banana soup made with heavy cream, swirls of strawberry purée, and a dollop of whipped cream on top. (It could have been a dessert.) The seafood salad, which included scallops, shrimp, and crabmeat, made a satisfying light lunch. Among other choices were a lamb sandwich with rosemary mayonnaise; a buffalo burger; grilled tuna with tarragon-papaya salsa; and blackened scallops with béarnaise sauce.

At dinner, we began with an excellent cold puréed apple soup and a creamy duck pâté. Here's a sampling of other appetizers: snails bourguignonne, linguine with a shellfish cream sauce, and Caesar salad. Plates are attractively decorated with fresh herbs and spices. The chef will prepare any fish that you catch—local fish are wahoo, yellowtail snapper, and dolphin (the fish). The rack of lamb is served with an out-of-the-ordinary raspberry sauce; the filet mignon comes with a Madeira sauce; and the swordfish is garnished with papaya coulis. The dessert of our choice was a puffed shell filled with cappuccino ice cream and topped with hot chocolate sauce. Other choices were a "black beast" cake (a rich chocolate pâté), amaretto or apple spice cheesecake, and a chocolate raspberry cake. For a special occasion, order the baked Alaska. And a word to the wise: Drink too many tasty Gumby Slumbers, the island's addictive frozen rum and fruit drinks that go down so easily when you're lying on the beach, and you won't have room for three meals a day.

Breakfast includes all the items you'd find in any top restaurant—freshly squeezed orange juice, fresh fruit, omelets, smoked salmon—plus some more unusual choices such as fresh catch of the day or eggs Benedict made with a crabcake.

Thirty suites, all with private bath. Mid-December through April, $635 (breakfast, lunch, dinner, and gratuity included for two) or $495 (room and gratuity only). At other times of the year, $450–$495 (breakfast, lunch, dinner, and gratuity included for two) or $335–$395 (room and gratuity only). Third person in the suite, $52 (no meals) or $126 (including meals). Lunch daily, 11:30 A.M. to 2:30 P.M., $25 prix fixe for outside guests; smaller meals are available for guests staying on the island. Dinner, 6:30 to 10:30 P.M., entrées, $20.50–$28. Thursday "gourmet night" dinner, $55; Sunday brunch, $28.50. Children under 12 not accepted. No pets. Mailing address: Route 4, Box 1036, Little Torch Key, FL 33042; (305) 872-2524; (800) 3-GET-LOST.

What to Do.   Included in the rates are use of the freshwater pool, sauna, exercise room, Hobie day sailers, Windsurfers, canoes, kayaks, snorkel gear, and fishing gear. Other activities are available for an additional fee. Snorkel trips to Looe Key to swim with the reef fish and to see the coral formations are popular. Guests can take a one-day scuba resort course or get certified in three to five days; go deep-sea fishing or flats fishing; charter the Hinkley Bermuda 40 or the 28-foot Sharpie for half-day or full-day sails. Or just relax in the hammock outside your suite.

If you begin to crave the crowds, Key West is less than one hour away. Music lovers can hear rock, folk, Dixieland, jazz, and Bahamian calypso bands perform in the many bars and clubs on famous Duval Street. There are walking tours and trolley tours of the Old Town. Tourists, vendors, and street performers gather each night in Mallory Square to celebrate the sunset.

How to Get There.   From Miami, take the Florida Turnpike to overseas highway U.S. 1 for approximately 120 miles to mile marker 28.5 on Little Torch Key. From Key West, take U.S. 1 north 28.5 miles to Little Torch Key. Turn right into Dolphin Marina to Little Palm Island Shore Station.

JANE STAUFFER

The Marquesa Hotel, *Key West, Florida*

The gentrification of Key West is exemplified by this elegant fifteen-room complex built before 1889. This property has been used as a drugstore, car dealership, grocery store, and until fairly recently, a flophouse. The Marquesa Hotel is the place to stay in Key West if you want to be in the historic district, but also want all the creature comforts of a first-class small hotel. A concierge is on duty twenty-four hours a day; there is room service and evening turndown service with Godiva chocolates placed by your bed. Each room has Belgian-cotton robes; a tray with a selection of bottled water, liquors, and snack items; and a security safe. There is also off-street parking. The interior landscaped courtyard has a large, heated swimming pool with a cascading fountain in the middle and is surrounded by plantings of palms, hibiscus, and jasmine.

The rooms are designer decorated in one of three coordinating wallpaper and fabric color schemes: green and beige, peach and blue, or yellow and green. All have wall-to-wall carpeting, marble tiled floors, and vanities in the baths, which have wonderful spotless glass shower doors. Rooms on the first and second floors have high ceilings and fans while the third-floor rooms have dormer windows and lower, angled ceilings. Standard rooms have a queen-size bed, top-quality Sony television, and reproduction antique bureaus and armoires. Room 3 is the largest standard room and faces the pool. Rooms 12 and 13 both have private balconies that overlook the courtyard. The deluxe rooms and suites (larger rooms) all have a small sitting area with a convertible couch and a television hidden in an armoire. Some of the rooms face the street, while others have views of the pool and the courtyard. All of the suites look out on the street. While we prefer the quiet of the interior rooms and the ability to open our door onto a deck overlooking the pool, guests like both types of rooms equally. A shower and changing rooms are available for guests who want to use the pool on the day they check out of their rooms.

Guests design their own breakfast with a choice of hot beverage; fruit plate or juice; granola; cheese plate with a baguette; sweet breads, croissants, or muffins. The meal is prepared by the restaurant and served in your room or outside by the pool. Selections from the dinner menu include sesame-encrusted rack of lamb with coconut-milk pesto, pan-seared yellowtail with pistachio crumbs, and grilled shrimp with black-bean salsa.

The manager told us that the hotel has hosted a number of weddings, which are usually held outdoors by the pool with the reception or dinner at the restaurant.

Eleven rooms and three suites, all with private bath. Late December through mid-April, $175–$250. Mid-April through May and late October through mid-December, $130–$195. June through late October, $110–$160. Continental breakfast, $6 additional per person. Children welcome. Third person in room,

$15 additional. No pets. 600 Fleming Street, Key West, FL 33040; (305) 292-1919; (800) 869-4631 or (305) 292-1919.

Where to Dine. The most sought-after tables at Louie's Backyard (700 Wassell Avenue; 305-294-0002) are those on the two outdoor levels overlooking the water. We enjoyed fried tortellini filled with chopped lamb, onions, and spices served with lentils and white raisins on a bed of arugula, radicchio, and leaf lettuce. The grouper had a crumb crust and was served with fettuccine tossed with conch, peppers, and herbs.

The owners of the Palm Grill, a tiny, casual neighborhood café deep in the heart of the Old Key West (1029 Southard Street; 305-296-1744) worked for years at the famous Quilted Giraffe restaurant in New York City. We enjoyed the salad of tabbouleh, baba ganoush, and hummus served on toasted pita and the red snapper grilled with pineapple salsa, topped with avocado aioli and garnished with marinated mushrooms, alfalfa sprouts, and scalloped potatoes. The key lime mousse is lighter and a little more sophisticated than traditional key lime pie.

For Cuban cuisine (remember, Key West is closer to Havana than to Miami), try the roast shredded pork cooked with garlic at El Siboney (900 Catherine Street; 305-296-4184).

Enjoy a late breakfast at one of the battered tables in the courtyard at Pepe's Café and Steak House, established in 1909, where you will get a good, reasonably priced meal and lots of casual Key West atmosphere (806 Caroline Street; 305-294-7100).

The 5 Brothers Grocery at 930 Southard Street is one of the last corner stores in Key West. Join the locals in the morning for café con leche (espresso with hot milk and sugar) and warm, buttered Cuban bread.

What to Do. There are enough bars along Duval Street, the one-mile central artery of town, for visitors to see Key West "on their hands and knees," as the locals like to say. Rock, folk, Dixieland, jazz, and Bahamian calypso bands can keep you singing and dancing from early afternoon to early morning. Take a trolley or walking tour of the Old Town and see more than 3,000 historic structures, including the house where Ernest Hemingway wrote *A Farewell to Arms* and *For Whom the Bell Tolls* in the 1930s. Bikes and motor scooters are available for rent. You also can go scuba diving, snorkeling, fishing, and sea kayaking. This is not the place to go if you are hoping to bask on a soft, sandy beach near the pounding ocean surf; the living coral reef that stretches 200 miles along the Keys separates the ocean from the coastline. Tourists, vendors, and street performers gather at Mallory Square each night to celebrate the sunset.

How to Get There.   Fly to Key West and take a taxi to the hotel. You won't need a car if you stay in Key West. From Miami, take U.S. 1 for 156 miles south to Key West.

APPENDIX

All of the Romantic Hideaways included in this book were reviewed in issues of our newsletter, "The Discerning Traveler," based on our personal visits. The choice of inns is ours alone; no one has paid to be included in this book. Further information about the areas in which each of these inns, bed and breakfasts, and hotels is located can be found in issues of "The Discerning Traveler"® and two guidebooks, *The Discerning Traveler's Guide to New England* and *The Discerning Traveler's Guide to the Middle Atlantic States*. This appendix cross-references each Romantic Hideaway to the appropriate book or issue of the newsletter. The books are published by St. Martin's Press and can be purchased at your local bookstore or ordered directly. The issues of the newsletter are available only from us. See the order form on the next page for books, back issues, or subscription information.

Romantic Hideaway	Publication where detailed information about the area can be found
Le Chateau Frontenac	V6N4 Quebec City and the Charlevoix Region
La Pinsonnière	V6N4 Quebec City and the Charlevoix Region
The Inn at Canoe Point	*The Discerning Traveler's Guide to New England*

The Blue Hill Inn	*The Discerning Traveler's Guide to New England*
The Keeper's House	*The Discerning Traveler's Guide to New England*
A Little Dream	V5N5 Mid-Coast Maine, Newcastle-Camden
Squire Tarbox Inn	V6N3 Mid-Coast Maine, Portland-Boothbay
The Inn at Harbor Head	V4N4 Kennebunkport, ME
The Captain Lord Mansion	V4N4 Kennebunkport, ME
Nestlenook Farm	V5N7 The White Mountains of New Hampshire
Rabbit Hill Inn	V5N7 The White Mountains of New Hampshire
Stowehof Inn	V4N7 Stowe, VT
Jackson House	*The Discerning Traveler's Guide to New England*
Cornucopia of Dorset	V5N4 Dorset, Manchester, Arlington, VT
1811 House	V5N4 Dorset, Manchester, Arlington, VT
Cliffwood Inn	*The Discerning Traveler's Guide to New England*
Wheatleigh	*The Discerning Traveler's Guide to New England*
Yankee Clipper Inn	V4N5 Cape Ann, Gloucester, Rockport, MA
Watermark Inn	*The Discerning Traveler's Guide to New England*
The Wauwinet	*The Discerning Traveler's Guide to New England*
Cliffside Inn	*The Discerning Traveler's Guide to New England*
Riverwind Inn	*The Discerning Traveler's Guide to New England*

Manor House	V6N5 Litchfield County, CT & Southern Berkshires
The Mayflower Inn	V6N5 Litchfield County, CT & Southern Berkshires
Troutbeck	V6N5 Litchfield County, CT & Southern Berkshires
Old Drovers Inn	V6N5 Litchfield County, CT & Southern Berkshires
Beekman Arms	*The Discerning Traveler's Guide to the Middle Atlantic States*
Inn New York City	Future Issue
Rose Inn	*The Discerning Traveler's Guide to the Middle Atlantic States*
The Whitehall Inn	V6N6 Lower Delaware River Valley, PA and NJ
Sweetwater Farm	*The Discerning Traveler's Guide to the Middle Atlantic States*
Smithton Inn	*The Discerning Traveler's Guide to the Middle Atlantic States*
Chestnut Hill on the Delaware	V6N6 Lower Delaware River Valley, PA and NJ
The Mainstay Inn	*The Discerning Traveler's Guide to the Middle Atlantic States*
The Queen Victoria	*The Discerning Traveler's Guide to the Middle Atlantic States*
Brampton	*The Discerning Traveler's Guide to the Middle Atlantic States*
The Inn at Perry Cabin	*The Discerning Traveler's Guide to the Middle Atlantic States*
Robert Morris Inn	*The Discerning Traveler's Guide to the Middle Atlantic States*
Mr. Mole Bed & Breakfast	V6N2 Baltimore, MD
Ashby Inn	*The Discerning Traveler's Guide to the Middle Atlantic States*

The Inn at Little Washington	*The Discerning Traveler's Guide to the Middle Atlantic States*	
Conyers House	*The Discerning Traveler's Guide to the Middle Atlantic States*	
Prospect Hill	V5N3	Charlottesville, VA & Blue Ridge Pky.
Williamsburg Inn	V4N3	Williamsburg, VA
The Swag	V4N6	The Great Smoky Mountains, NC
Pine Crest Inn	V4N6	The Great Smoky Mountains, NC
The Greystone Inn	V4N6	The Great Smoky Mountains, NC
Two Meeting Street	V5N8	Charleston, SC
Kiawah Island Inn	V5N8	Charleston, SC
Cheeca Lodge	V4N8	Key West, FL
Little Palm Island	V4N8	Key West, FL
The Marquesa Hotel	V4N8	Key West, FL

Subscription, Book, and Back-Issue Order Form

The Discerning Traveler,® the East Coast's premier travel newsletter, has published over forty in-depth guides to destinations from Maine and eastern Canada to Florida. For more information about the areas near these fifty-two romantic hideaways, get the corresponding issues of the newsletter and guidebooks (see appendix). Each newsletter issue or book chapter includes suggestions on what to do, at least a dozen places to stay and dine, budget, itinerary, map, reading list, recipe, special events, history, and illustrations. Subscribers get a toll-free 800 number to ask questions of the staff about any of the destinations covered in past issues.

Subscription Offers

One-year subscription to *The Discerning Traveler* ®
(6 issues) . . . . $50.00 $_____
Two-year subscription (12 issues) includes a
Discerning Traveler ® binder. . . . . $100.00 $_____

Back-Issue Orders

Attach list of issues desired, using numbers from the appendix.
Subscribers may purchase back issues at $4.00 each—50% off
    the regular price.
I am subscribing and would like to order ____ back issues $_____
    listed at $4.00 each
I am not subscribing but would like to order ____ back issues $_____
    listed at $8.00 each

Total above $_____
Pennsylvania residents add 7% state and local sales tax $_____

Total $_____

Call Toll-Free (800) 673-7834

Payment enclosed (make check payable to *The Discerning Traveler* ®)
Charge to: VISA   MasterCard

Acct. No._____ Expiration Date_____

Signature_____

Name_____

Address_____

City_____ State_____ Zip_____

(continued on next page)

Send to: *The Discerning Traveler*
504 West Mermaid Lane
Philadelphia, PA 19118
(800) 673-7834   (215) 247-5578

Canadian subscriptions $60.
Other countries $65.
Foreign back-issue orders add $5.00 postage.

Send for a free map of destinations reviewed by *The Discerning Traveler*®.

The Discerning Traveler's Guide to New England and *The Discerning Traveler's Guide to the Middle Atlantic States* are available in local bookstores or may be ordered through Publisher's Book & Audio, P.O. Box 070059, 5446 Arthur Kill Road, Staten Island, NY 10307; 1-800-288-2131.

Discounts are available for orders of ten or more books; call 1-800-221-7945, ext. 645.